INTERFACT
REFERENCE

THE BOOK AND DISK THAT WORK TOGETHER

ATLAS

TWO
CAN
™

What's in the book?

What is an atlas?   4

Hot and cold   6

About this atlas   8

World map   10

The Arctic and
Antarctica   12

Canada   14

The United States   16

Mexico, Central America
and the Caribbean   18

South America   20

Northern Europe   22

Southern Europe   24

Russia and its
neighbours   26

The Middle East   28

Northern Africa   30

Southern Africa   32

Southern Asia   34

Eastern Asia   36

South-east Asia   38

Australia, New Zealand
and the Pacific Islands   40

Gazetteer   42

Index   44

Troubleshooting tips   48

What's on the disk?

First of all, you have to collect your Interfact passport. Follow the instructions on screen. Then explore the interactive maps and use the Picture Index to discover fascinating facts about the world's animals, plants, peoples and places. As you travel the globe, be sure to visit the capital cities – some of them feature fun activities and exciting adventures (see right).

There are 16 interactive maps to explore.

Installing the Atlas CD-ROM

See page 48 for troubleshooting tips, system requirements and helpline details.

Windows 95 or 98
The Atlas program should start automatically when you put the CD into your CD-ROM drive. If it does not, follow these instructions.
1. Put the CD into the CD drive.
2. Double-click on My Computer.
3. Double-click on the CD drive icon.
4. Double-click on the ATLAS icon.

Windows 3.1 or 3.11
1. Put the CD into the CD Drive.
2. Open File Manager.
3. Double-click on the CD drive icon.
4. Double-click on the ATLAS icon.

Macintosh
1. Put the CD into the CD drive.
2. Double-click on the ATLAS FOR MAC icon.

Power Macintosh
1. Put the CD into the CD drive.
2. Double-click on the ATLAS FOR POWER MAC icon.

Virtual Globe

Take a closer look at the world using a stunning 3-D globe and answer quick-fire questions on the continents.
Location: Canberra

Find Agatha

Track down your long-lost Aunt Agatha using the book to solve the clues in the postcards she sends you.
Location: Washington DC

World Class

Find the answers to all your questions about map-making and geography – this teacher is in a class of her own!
Location: Brasília

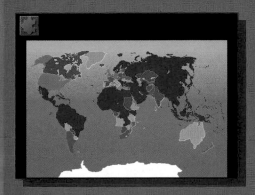

Jig Map

Pick up the pieces and put the world back together with these interactive jigsaws. Once each jigsaw is finished, click away to find out more!
Location: Tokyo

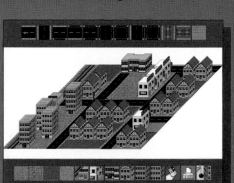

Map Maker

Create your own maps on screen. Print them out to keep or put your map-reading skills to the test and help Agatha find her missing handbag.
Location: Cairo

Picture Index

There are over 400 interesting pictures in your Atlas. Use the Picture Index to find out more about each one – from Antarctic cod to desert lizards!
Location: Toolbar

The Toolbar

The toolbar appears whenever you move the cursor to the right-hand edge of the screen.

 Click here to return to the main screen

 Click here to go to the Picture Index

 Click here to see activities completed

 Click here to see your passport

 Click here to use the note pad

 Click here to go to the gift shop

 Click here for help

 Click here to quit

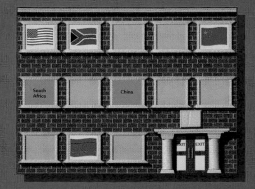

Windows on the World

A mad memory challenge to test your knowledge. You'll be racing against the clock to match up countries with their capital cities, currencies, languages and flags!
Location: Moscow

Around the World in 80 Days

Help Phileas and Passepartout navigate their way around the world. Visit more than 150 capital cities along the way.
Location: London

What is an atlas?

An atlas is a book of maps showing different parts of the world. Maps are small pictures of big places drawn from above. They can show somewhere as small as a village or as big as the world. You can use atlases and maps in all sorts of ways. They might show you how to find your way around, or tell you what a place is like.

1 One of the most difficult maps to draw is one showing all of the world. This is because the world is round, like a huge ball, but maps are flat. Imagine painting the world on to the skin of an orange.

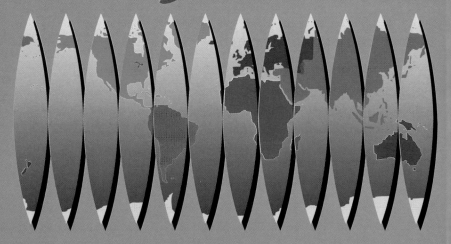

2 You could carefully peel the skin into segments.

3 Then you could lay the peel flat to make a map of the world.

ARCTIC OCEAN

Arctic Circle

NORTH AMERICA

EUROPE

ASIA

PACIFIC OCEAN

ATLANTIC OCEAN

AFRICA

Equator

INDIAN OCEAN

SOUTH AMERICA

AUSTRALIA

ANTARCTICA

Antarctic Circle

4 Mapmakers fill the gaps by stretching some parts of the map and squashing others.

On this map, you can see that more than half of the Earth is covered by four big oceans. The rest of the Earth is divided into seven huge areas of land, called continents. There are also three imaginary lines on the map. The equator circles the Earth's middle. The Arctic Circle is at the top of the Earth and the Antarctic Circle is at the bottom.

Different kinds of maps show different amounts of detail, but most maps show places much smaller than they really are.

1 This is a picture of a house on the corner of Park Street, which runs through a sea-side town. You can see the hedge around the house, the tree outside and some of the street, but you cannot see the town or the sea because the picture is not big enough to show all these details.

2 This map shows Park Street as if drawn from above. It shows less detail but a bigger area than the last picture. Can you spot the house on the corner? On this map, Park Street measures 10cm, but it is really 1km long. This means that on the map every 10cm is the same as 1km in the real place. This is called scale.

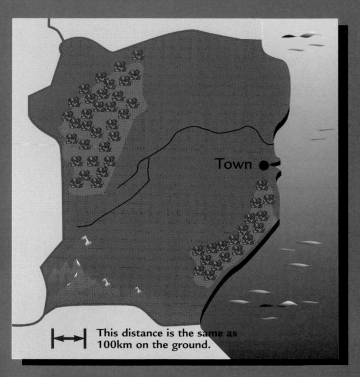

This distance is the same as 100km on the ground.

3 This map shows a bigger area than the last map because it has a smaller scale. It shows all of the town. Look how close it is to the sea. You cannot see the houses or all the streets, but you can see Park Street. On this map, Park Street is 5cm long. This means every 5cm on the map is the same as 1km in the real place.

4 This map shows the country where the town is found. Now the town is only shown by a black dot. The scale bar tells you that 1cm on the map is the same as 100km in the real place. In this atlas, each map has a different scale and scale bar. On pages 10-11 you can see all the countries of the world at the same scale.

Hot and cold

Around the world, there are different patterns of weather called climates. The climate of a country depends on where it is in the world. It is always hot near the equator and cold near the North and South Poles. On each map in this atlas, you will find a locator globe, showing you where countries and continents are in the world. The globe has arrows pointing to the four directions – north, south, east and west.

The sun warms all the countries in the world, but shines more strongly on some than others. These countries have the warmest weather. Around the world, the weather also changes at different times of year.

Around the North and South Poles, the sun is never high in the sky and shines weakly, so the land is always cold, especially in winter.

Near the equator, the sun shines strongest and directly from above. Here the climate is hot, with wet and dry seasons.

Above and below the equator, there are two imaginary lines called the Tropic of Cancer and the Tropic of Capricorn. Countries between the tropics and the North and South Poles have warm summers and cold winters.

Different climates suit particular kinds of plants, and make different types of land for animals and people to live in. If a place has a rainy climate, lots of plants grow. If the climate is dry, fewer and different plants grow.

On the map below and the maps in this atlas, different types of land are shown by small pictures, called symbols, and colours. These photographs show you what the land really looks like.

Usually, the poles are icy cold. In summer, a few small plants grow around the Arctic.

Deciduous forests grow in cool areas. The trees lose their leaves in autumn.

Evergreen trees stay green all year. Evergreen forests grow in cold places.

Grassland includes tropical savannah (seen here), farmland and flat plains, called pampas.

Only the toughest plants and animals are able to survive in dry deserts.

Thick, green rainforests grow where it is warm and wet all year.

Few plants grow on rocky mountains, which are often covered in snow.

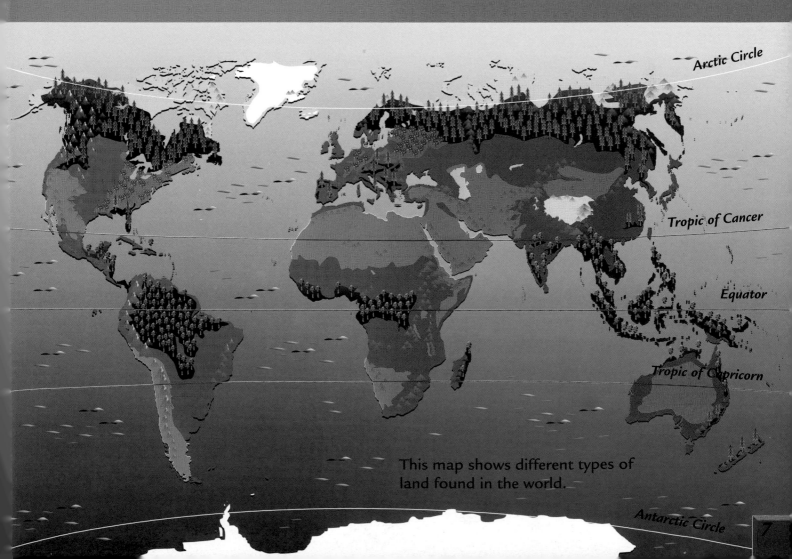

Arctic Circle

Tropic of Cancer

Equator

Tropic of Capricorn

This map shows different types of land found in the world.

Antarctic Circle

About this atlas

The maps in this atlas can tell you an enormous amount about the places they show. Look carefully at the pictures to find out more.

Crops grow all over the world. Look out for wheat, rice, fruit and vegetables. You may see coffee, tea and sugar cane, too.

Each country is run from a capital city. These are shown by the flag of the country and a star.

Some buildings are shown on the maps. You may see a famous monument, an old ruin or a type of home.

A grey line shows a country border. When countries are arguing about a border or are not sure where the border is, the line is dotted.

This picture shows where people drill into the land and seabed for oil, which is used to power all kinds of machines.

A blue line shows a river. The name of the river is written alongside. Rivers can run through many countries.

Different kinds of animals live in different parts of the world. Look for animals that live in the sea, on land and in the air.

This picture shows where people mine for diamonds. People also mine coal, silver, jewels, gold, copper, tin and iron.

Different people live around the world. Look for people playing sport or enjoying a traditional dance.

Royal gramma fish

Oil

VENEZUELA

Rice

Rice

Diamonds

Georgetown
GUYANA

Paramaribo

SURINAM

Cayenne

FRENCH GUIANA (France)

Gold

Gold

Angel Falls

Diamonds

Gold

Equator

Crocodile

Emerald tree boa

Piranha fish

B R A Z I L

Gold

Tobacco

Sugar cane

Cotton

Cargo ships

Dug-out canoes

River Amazon

Toucan

Recife

Oil

Stilt house

Diamonds

Gold

bird

Rainforest clearing

River São Francisco

Oil

Shrimp

Jaguar

Vampire bat

Iron

Cotton

Gold

Corn

Brasília

Tourism

Lobster

BOLIVIA

Gold

Rice

Oranges

La Paz

Cotton

Wheat

Cotton

Iron

ANDES MOUNTAINS

Potatoes

Gas

Cattle ranching

Carnival

1
2
3
4
5
6
7
8

8   E   F   G   H   I   J   K   L   M

About the Factfile

Each map has a Factfile with facts about the places you can see. You might find out about a special animal or plant from a particular part of the world. Look at the picture beside each fact and then find it on the map. The facts in this Factfile are about the map of part of South America shown on the opposite page. Can you find all the pictures on the map?

On page 42, you will find a gazetteer, full of all different kinds of facts about the countries of the world.

Factfile

 South America is home to nearly one quarter of all known animals and around 2,500 different kinds of trees.

 The longest mountain range in the world is the Andes in South America.

Half of all the people in South America live in Brazil.

▼ This girl is answering the Fact Finder question. She is using a ruler and her finger to find the correct grid reference.

 FACT FINDER

Each map has a grid, which divides it into squares. The columns run up and down and have letters. The rows run from side to side and have numbers. This means each square has a name, or grid reference.

The Fact Finder asks questions about places on the map. You can find the answers by looking at the grid reference.

Here is a Fact Finder question about the map of part of South America shown on the opposite page.

▶ What is the name of the highest waterfall in the world? (See square E 4.)

To find square E 4, lay your ruler on column E, at the bottom of the map. Leave the ruler lying on the map. Now put your finger on row 4, at the side of the map. Run your finger along row 4 in a straight line. Square E 4 is where your finger meets the ruler.

You should have found Angel Falls which is in Venezuela.

World map

ARCTIC
OCEAN

GREENLAND
(Denmark)

ALASKA (USA)

CANADA

FINLAND   NORWAY

ICELAND   THE
                NETHERLANDS   SWEDEN

                                   ESTONIA
                                   LATVIA

UNITED STATES   UNITED
OF AMERICA   KINGDOM

REPUBLIC
OF IRELAND

BELGIUM

ATLANTIC
OCEAN

FRANCE

ANDORRA

SPAIN

PORTUGAL

These countries in
Europe are
shown more
clearly inside
the circle on
page 11.

AZORES
(Portugal)

MADEIRA
(Portugal)   MOROCCO

BALEARIC
ISLANDS
(Spain)   TUNISIA   MALTA

CRETE
(Greece)

BERMUDA (UK)

DOMINICAN REPUBLIC
PUERTO RICO (USA)
VIRGIN ISLANDS (USA & UK)
ANGUILLA (UK)
ST KITTS & NEVIS
ANTIGUA & BARBUDA
GUADELOUPE (France)
DOMINICA
MARTINIQUE (France)
ST LUCIA
BARBADOS
GRENADA
TRINIDAD & TOBAGO

CANARY
ISLANDS
(Spain)

ALGERIA   LIBYA

WESTERN
SAHARA

MEXICO

BAHAMAS

CUBA

BELIZE

JAMAICA

GUATEMALA
HONDURAS   HAITI

EL SALVADOR

NICARAGUA

MONTSERRAT (UK)

ST VINCENT &
THE GRENADINES

COSTA RICA

PANAMA

VENEZUELA

GUYANA

SURINAM

COLOMBIA

FRENCH
GUIANA
(France)

GALAPAGOS
ISLANDS
(Ecuador)

ECUADOR

PERU

BRAZIL

PACIFIC
OCEAN

BOLIVIA

PARAGUAY

CAPE
VERDE
ISLANDS

MAURITANIA   MALI

SENEGAL

GAMBIA

GUINEA-
BISSAU   GUINEA

SIERRA
LEONE

LIBERIA

NIGER

BURKINA
FASO

IVORY
COAST

GHANA

BENIN

TOGO

NIGERIA

CHAD

CENTRAL
AFRICAN
REPUBLIC

CAMEROON

SÃO TOMÉ & PRÍNCIPE

EQUATORIAL
GUINEA

GABON

DEMOCRA
REPUBLI
OF CONG

CONGO

CABINDA
(Angola)

ANGOLA

ZAMB

NAMIBIA

BOTSWANA

ATLANTIC
OCEAN

REPUBLIC OF
SOUTH AFRICA

LESOTHO

The world is divided into
almost 200 countries and
this map shows most of
them. The countries are
different colours so that
you can tell them apart.
Some countries own places
in other parts of the world.
In this atlas, these kinds of
places have two labels. One
label gives their name and another
label in brackets gives the name of
the country that owns them.

CHILE

URUGUAY

ARGENTINA

FALKLAND
ISLANDS
(UK)

SOUTH
GEORGIA
(UK)

ANTARCTICA

RUSSIA

KAZAKHSTAN

UKRAINE

AZERBAIJAN

ARMENIA

GEORGIA

TURKEY

CYPRUS

SYRIA

LEBANON

JORDAN

ISRAEL

EGYPT

SUDAN

UZBEKISTAN

TURKMENISTAN

KYRGYZSTAN

TAJIKISTAN

AFGHANISTAN

IRAN

IRAQ

KUWAIT

BAHRAIN

QATAR

UNITED
ARAB
EMIRATES

SAUDI
ARABIA

OMAN

MONGOLIA

CHINA

BHUTAN

NEPAL

PAKISTAN

INDIA

MYANMAR

NORTH
KOREA

JAPAN

SOUTH
KOREA

PACIFIC
OCEAN

MACAU
(Portugal)

TAIWAN
(China)

HONG
KONG
(China)

LAOS

VIETNAM

THAILAND

CAMBODIA

BANGLADESH

ANDAMAN
ISLANDS
(India)

NICOBAR
ISLANDS
(India)

ERITREA

YEMEN

DJIBOUTI

SOCOTRA
(Yemen)

ETHIOPIA

SOMALIA

UGANDA

KENYA

RWANDA

BURUNDI

TANZANIA

MALAWI

COMOROS

MAYOTTE (France)

MALDIVE
ISLANDS

SRI
LANKA

INDIAN
OCEAN

SINGAPORE

SEYCHELLES

MALAYSIA

I N D O N E S I A

PHILIPPINES

BRUNEI

PALAU
(USA)

GUAM (USA)

NORTHERN
MARIANAS
(USA)

MARSHALL
ISLANDS

STATES OF MICRONESIA

NAURU

KIRIBATI

IRIAN JAYA
(Indonesia)

PAPUA NEW
GUINEA

SOLOMON
ISLANDS

TUVALU

VANUATU

FIJI

AUSTRALIA

NEW
CALEDONIA
(France)

ZIMBABWE

MOZAMBIQUE

MADAGASCAR

SWAZILAND

TASMANIA
(Australia)

NEW ZEALAND

SWEDEN

LATVIA

DENMARK

LITHUANIA

(Russia)

BELARUS

GERMANY

POLAND

LUXEMBOURG

CZECH
REPUBLIC

SLOVAKIA

UKRAINE

LIECHTENSTEIN

AUSTRIA

HUNGARY

MOLDOVA

SWITZERLAND

SLOVENIA

ROMANIA

MONACO

SAN
MARINO

CROATIA

FEDERAL
REPUBLIC OF
YUGOSLAVIA

BOSNIA-
HERZEGOVINA

BULGARIA

CORSICA
(France)

ITALY

MACEDONIA

TURKEY

SARDINIA
(Italy)

VATICAN
CITY

ALBANIA

GREECE

SICILY
(Italy)

Some countries in Europe are
crowded together. In this circle,
we have made these countries
bigger so that you can see
them more easily.

The Arctic

The Arctic is the part of the world that lies closest to the North Pole. Around the Pole, the Arctic Ocean is frozen all year, but further away the ice and snow melt in the summer. In winter, the sun hardly shines which makes the Arctic very cold. Very little grows there, except for a few small plants such as moss or lichen.

FACT FINDER

▶ Which Arctic animal weighs more than nine grown men and lives on the moving ice? (See square F 8.)

▶ Which bird travels further than any other bird in the world? Every year it flies over 13,000km from the North to the South Pole? (See square F 7.)

▶ What do Arctic peoples often use to travel across the ice? (See E 8.)

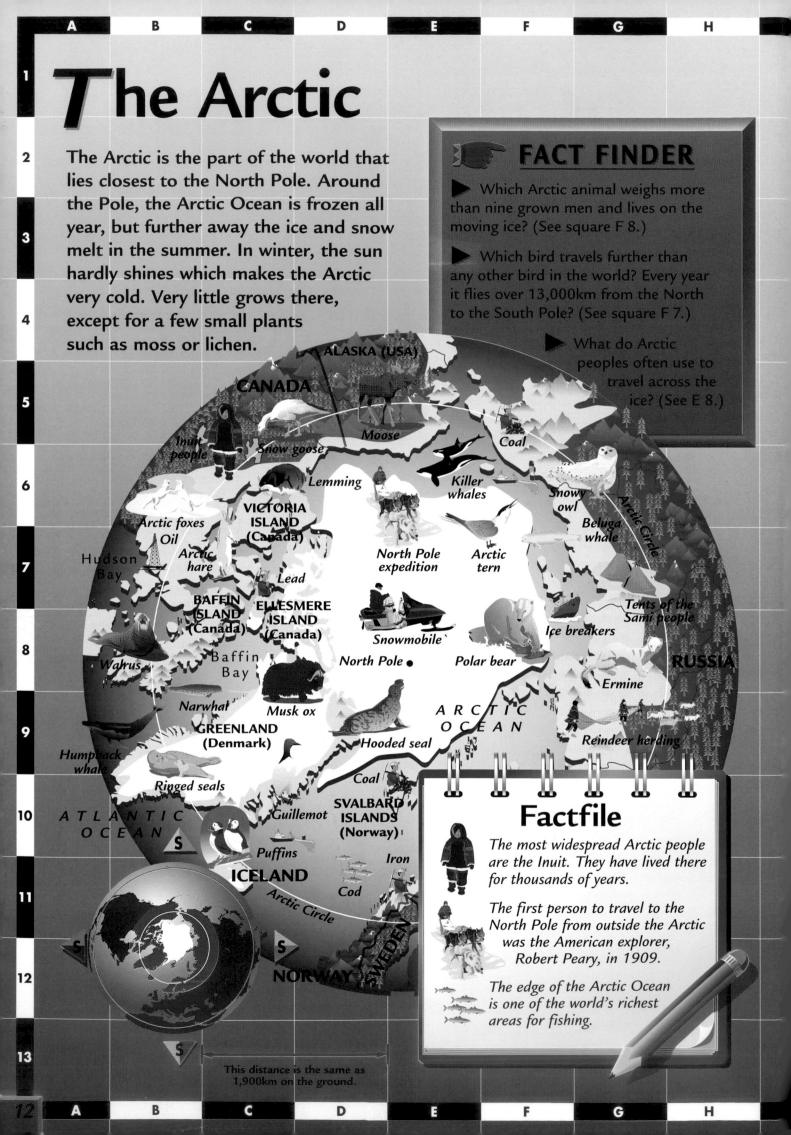

ALASKA (USA)

CANADA

Inuit people

Snow goose

Moose

Coal

Lemming

Killer whales

Snowy owl

Arctic Circle

Arctic foxes

Oil

VICTORIA ISLAND (Canada)

Beluga whale

Hudson Bay

Arctic hare

Lead

North Pole expedition

Arctic tern

BAFFIN ISLAND (Canada)

ELLESMERE ISLAND (Canada)

Tents of the Sami people

Ice breakers

Snowmobile

Walrus

Baffin Bay

North Pole •

Polar bear

RUSSIA

Ermine

Narwhal

Musk ox

A R C T I C O C E A N

GREENLAND (Denmark)

Hooded seal

Reindeer herding

Humpback whale

Ringed seals

Coal

ATLANTIC OCEAN

Guillemot

SVALBARD ISLANDS (Norway)

Iron

Puffins

Cod

ICELAND

Arctic Circle

NORWAY

SWEDEN

This distance is the same as 1,900km on the ground.

Factfile

The most widespread Arctic people are the Inuit. They have lived there for thousands of years.

The first person to travel to the North Pole from outside the Arctic was the American explorer, Robert Peary, in 1909.

The edge of the Arctic Ocean is one of the world's richest areas for fishing.

Antarctica

Antarctica is an enormous ice-covered continent near the South Pole. It is the coldest and windiest place on Earth. Few animals live around the pole but there are seals and birds on the coast, and plants and fish in the sea. The only people living in Antarctica are scientists. They stay on research stations to study the land and its wildlife.

Factfile

In 1911, Roald Amundsen, a Norwegian explorer, became the first person to reach the South Pole.

Up to 30,000 tourists a year cruise the waters around Antarctica to see the land and its wildlife.

Antarctica has many icebergs. The largest one ever found was three times the size of the island of Cyprus.

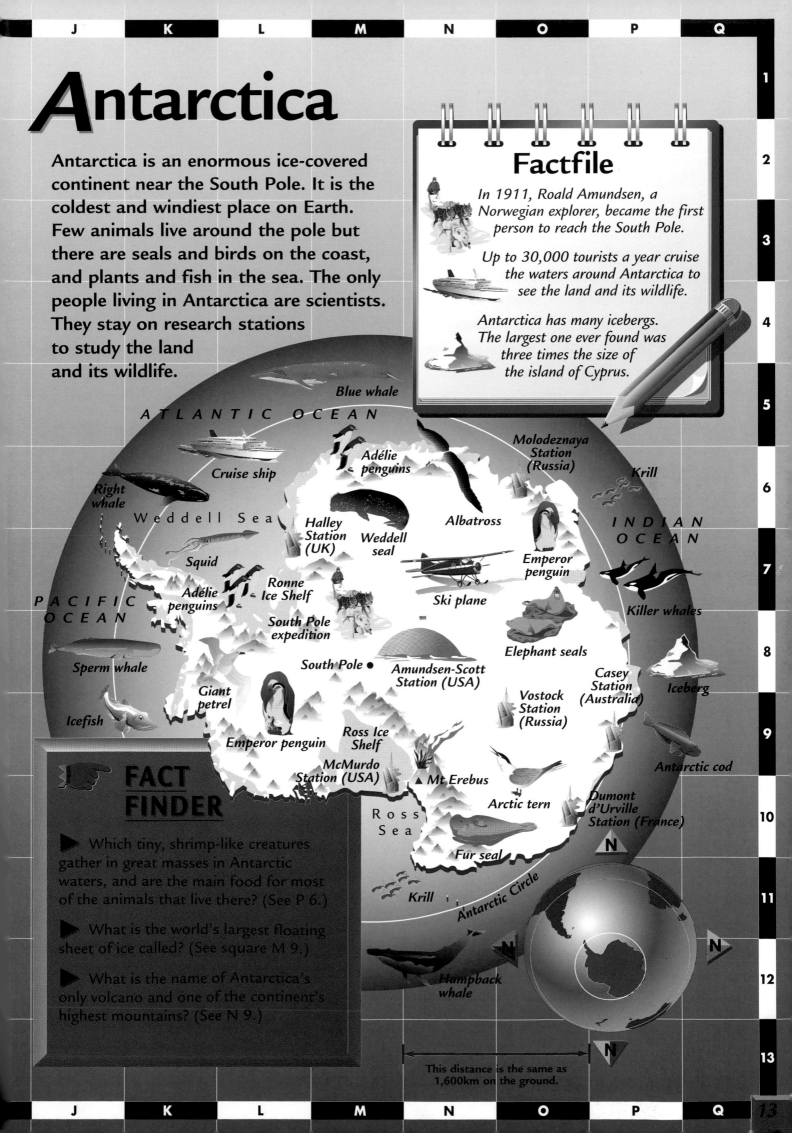

Blue whale

ATLANTIC OCEAN

Cruise ship

Adélie penguins

Molodeznaya Station (Russia)

Krill

Right whale

Weddell Sea

Halley Station (UK)

Weddell seal

Albatross

INDIAN OCEAN

Squid

Emperor penguin

Adélie penguins

Ronne Ice Shelf

Ski plane

Killer whales

PACIFIC OCEAN

South Pole expedition

Sperm whale

Elephant seals

South Pole ●

Amundsen-Scott Station (USA)

Casey Station (Australia)

Iceberg

Giant petrel

Vostock Station (Russia)

Icefish

Emperor penguin

Ross Ice Shelf

McMurdo Station (USA)

▲ Mt Erebus

Antarctic cod

Ross Sea

Arctic tern

Dumont d'Urville Station (France)

Fur seal

Krill

Antarctic Circle

Humpback whale

N

FACT FINDER

▶ Which tiny, shrimp-like creatures gather in great masses in Antarctic waters, and are the main food for most of the animals that live there? (See P 6.)

▶ What is the world's largest floating sheet of ice called? (See square M 9.)

▶ What is the name of Antarctica's only volcano and one of the continent's highest mountains? (See N 9.)

This distance is the same as 1,600km on the ground.

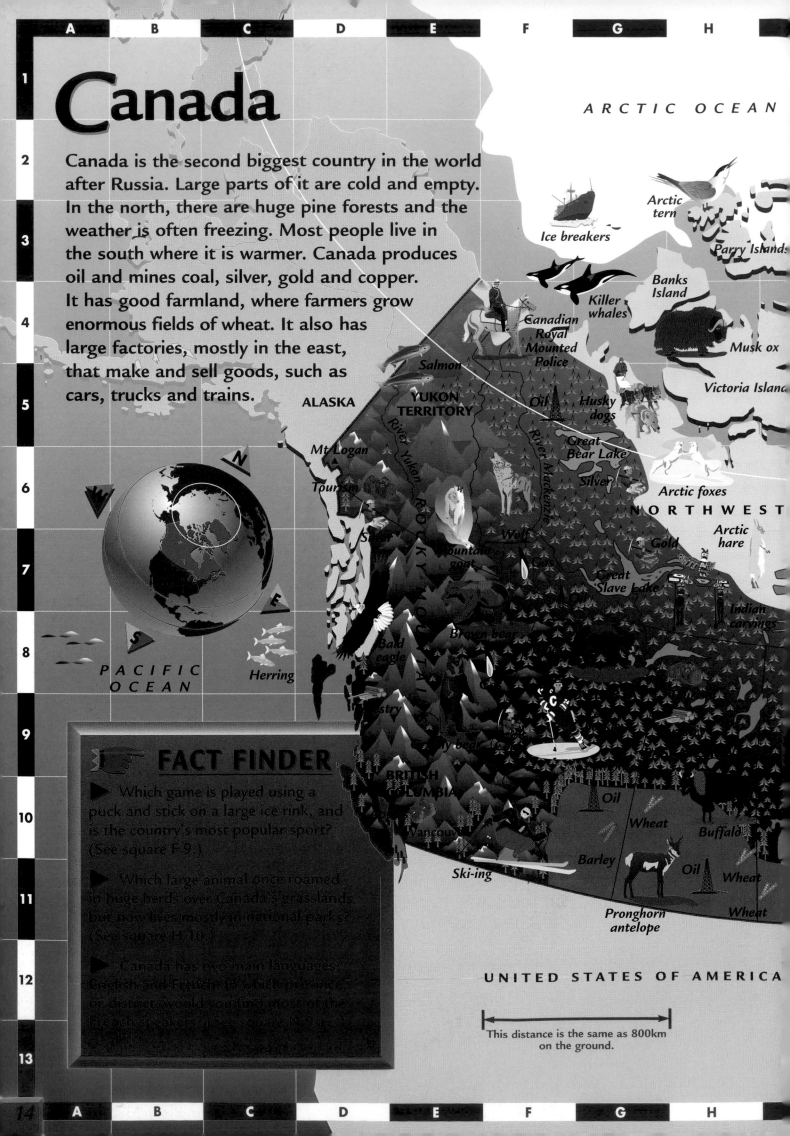

1

2

Canada

Canada is the second biggest country in the world after Russia. Large parts of it are cold and empty. In the north, there are huge pine forests and the weather is often freezing. Most people live in the south where it is warmer. Canada produces oil and mines coal, silver, gold and copper. It has good farmland, where farmers grow enormous fields of wheat. It also has large factories, mostly in the east, that make and sell goods, such as cars, trucks and trains.

ARCTIC OCEAN

Ice breakers

Arctic tern

Parry Islands

Banks Island

Killer whales

Musk ox

Victoria Island

Canadian Royal Mounted Police

Salmon

ALASKA

YUKON TERRITORY

Oil

Husky dogs

River Yukon

Great Bear Lake

Silver

Mt Logan

Tourism

Arctic foxes

NORTHWEST

Arctic hare

River Mackenzie

ROCKY

Wolf

Gold

Mountain goat

Gas

Great Slave Lake

Indian carvings

Brown bear

Bald eagle

PACIFIC OCEAN

Herring

MOUNTAINS

FACT FINDER

▶ Which game is played using a puck and stick on a large ice rink, and is the country's most popular sport? (See square F 9.)

▶ Which large animal once roamed in huge herds over Canada's grasslands but now lives mostly in national parks? (See square H 10.)

▶ Canada has two main languages, English and French. In which province or district would you find most of the French speakers? (See square N 9.)

BRITISH COLUMBIA

Vancouver

Ski-ing

Oil

Wheat

Buffalo

Barley

Oil

Wheat

Pronghorn antelope

Wheat

UNITED STATES OF AMERICA

This distance is the same as 800km on the ground.

1
2
3
4
5
6
7
8
9
10
11
12
13

Ellesmere
Island

Queen
Elizabeth Islands

Lemming

GREENLAND
(Denmark)

Walrus

Beluga whale

Hooded seal

Narwhal

Prince
of Wales
Island

Inuit
people

Baffin Island

Snowy
owl

Snowmobile

Arctic Circle

Polar bear

Factfile

Pine forests cover more than
one-third of Canada. The trees
are cut down by lumberjacks and
made into timber and paper.

Canada is famous for its sweet
maple syrup. It is made in the
spring from the sticky sap of
sugar maple trees.

In Canada no one is far from water.
The country has over one million
lakes. Lake Superior, on the
border between Canada and
the United States, is the
largest freshwater lake
in the world.

T E R R I T O R I E S

Starfish

Humpback whale

A T L A N T I C
O C E A N

Canada geese

Ice breakers

Lynx

Iron

Puffins

Right whale

Moose

H u d s o n
B a y

Mink

Snow goose

Float plane

NEWFOUNDLAND

Cod

MANITOBA

QUEBEC

Iron

Forestry

Making
paper

Forestry

Maple
syrup

Gold

Copper

Gulf
of
St Lawrence

Tourist bus

NEW
BRUNSWICK

Dairy
cattle

Potatoes

NOVA SCOTIA

Apples

eef cattle

Lake Superior

Ottawa

PRINCE
EDWARD
ISLAND

Blue whale

CN

Car building

Lake
Huron

Lake Ontario

Pigs

Lake
Michigan

Lake Erie

Niagara Falls

Lobster

The United States

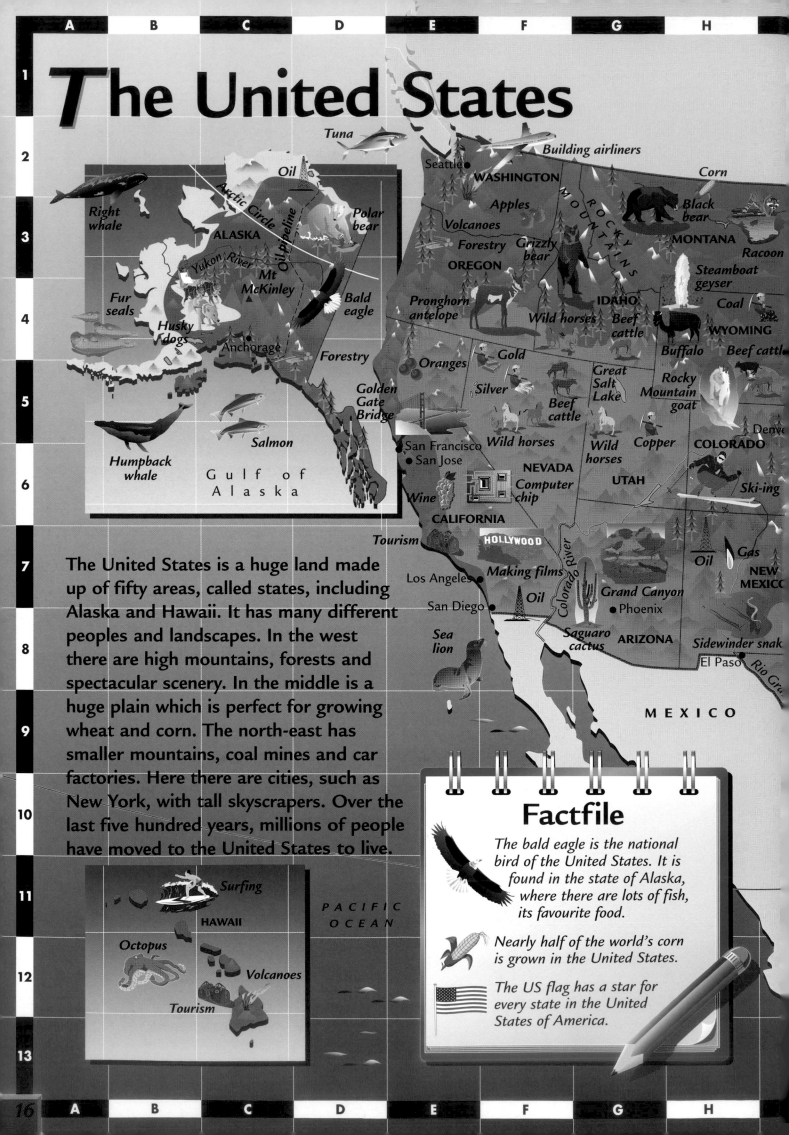

Tuna

Building airliners

Corn

Seattle

WASHINGTON

Apples

Oil

Right whale

Volcanoes

Black bear

ALASKA

Forestry

Grizzly bear

MONTANA

Racoon

Yukon River

OREGON

Steamboat geyser

Fur seals

Mt McKinley

Pronghorn antelope

IDAHO

Coal

Husky dogs

Wild horses

Beef cattle

WYOMING

Anchorage

Bald eagle

Oranges

Gold

Buffalo

Beef cattl

Forestry

Silver

Great Salt Lake

Rocky Mountain goat

Golden Gate Bridge

Beef cattle

Wild horses

Copper

COLORADO

Salmon

San Francisco

Wild horses

Denv

Humpback whale

San Jose

NEVADA

UTAH

Gulf of Alaska

Computer chip

Ski-ing

Wine

CALIFORNIA

HOLLYWOOD

Tourism

Oil

Gas

Making films

NEW MEXICO

The United States is a huge land made up of fifty areas, called states, including Alaska and Hawaii. It has many different peoples and landscapes. In the west there are high mountains, forests and spectacular scenery. In the middle is a huge plain which is perfect for growing wheat and corn. The north-east has smaller mountains, coal mines and car factories. Here there are cities, such as New York, with tall skyscrapers. Over the last five hundred years, millions of people have moved to the United States to live.

Los Angeles

San Diego

Oil

Grand Canyon

Phoenix

Sea lion

Saguaro cactus

ARIZONA

Sidewinder snak

El Paso

Rio Gra

MEXICO

Surfing

PACIFIC OCEAN

HAWAII

Octopus

Volcanoes

Tourism

Factfile

The bald eagle is the national bird of the United States. It is found in the state of Alaska, where there are lots of fish, its favourite food.

Nearly half of the world's corn is grown in the United States.

The US flag has a star for every state in the United States of America.

CANADA

This distance is the same as 800km on the ground.

Oil

NORTH DAKOTA

Wheat

Gas   Corn

SOUTH DAKOTA

Mt Rushmore

Cargo ships

MINNESOTA

Iron

Wheat

Corn

WISCONSIN

Dairy cattle

Dairy cattle

Milwaukee

Berries

Berries

MICHIGAN

Car building

Detroit

Cargo ships

Niagara Falls

VERMONT

Dairy cattle

NEW YORK

Dairy cattle

New York

Cleveland

PENNSYLVANIA

The Capitol

Washington DC

WEST VIRGINIA

MAINE

Forestry

Moose

NEW HAMPSHIRE

MASSACHUSETTS

Boston

RHODE ISLAND

CONNECTICUT

Statue of Liberty

NEW JERSEY

Philadelphia

Baltimore

DELAWARE

MARYLAND

Prairie dogs

NEBRASKA

Wheat

Corn

Beef cattle

Pigs

IOWA

Tractor building

ILLINOIS

Sears Tower

Chicago

Gateway Arch

St Louis

INDIANA

Indianapolis

Columbus

OHIO

Corn

Coal

Ohio River

Coal

VIRGINIA

Tobacco

Beef cattle

Kansas City

KANSAS

Sunflowers   Wheat

MISSOURI

Iron

Skunk

Missouri River

KENTUCKY

Country music

Nashville

NORTH CAROLINA

Cotton

APPALACHIAN MOUNTAINS

Right whale

ATLANTIC OCEAN

Wheat

Oklahoma City

OKLAHOMA

Coyote

Cotton

Memphis

TENNESSEE

ARKANSAS

Cotton

ALABAMA

Cotton

MISSISSIPPI

SOUTH CAROLINA

GEORGIA

Peanuts

Lobster

Cotton

Mississippi River

Beef cattle

Dallas

Fort Worth

Cowboys

LOUISIANA

Mansion house

Jacksonville

Kennedy Space Center

Oil   Oil   Gas

Austin

TEXAS

San Antonio

Houston

Jazz music

Paddle steamer

New Orleans

Gas

Oil

Alligator

Oranges

FLORIDA

Dolphin

Scuba diving

Beef cattle

Oil

Lobster

Lemons

Oranges

N

W   **E**

S

Gulf of Mexico

Tropic of Cancer

FACT FINDER

▶ Where would you find a famous geyser that spurts a jet of hot water 30m into the sky once every hour? (See square H 3.)

▶ Which mountain in South Dakota, North America has huge faces of four US presidents carved into it? (See square I 4.)

▶ What is the name of the Chicago tower, which is 443m tall, has 110 floors and is one of the highest buildings in the world? (See square M 5.)

Mexico, Central America and the Caribbean

Saguaro cactus

BAJA CALIFORNIA

SIERRA MADRE

UNITED STATES
OF AMERICA

Beef
cattle

Cotton

Silver

Sea lion

Rice

Coyote

Elephant seals

Rio Grande

Armadillo

Gulf of Mexico

Beef
cattle

Cotton

MEXICO

Grapefruit

Lobster

Anchovies

Blue whale

P A C I F I C
O C E A N

Spectacled
bear

Lemons

Tobacco

Corn

Oranges

Humpback whale

Corn

Shrimp

Chichén
Itzá

Tourism

Polka dot
grouper fish

Tourism

Forestry

Iron

Corn

Oil

Mexico City

Scarlet
macaw

Spider
monkey

Factfile

Mexico is one of the world's
biggest producers of silver.

The Caribbean Islands are some
of the world's most popular
holiday places. Cruise ships
carry passengers from one
island to another.

Honduras is one of the world's
largest producers of bananas.
The fruit is green when it is
picked, but ripens as it is
shipped across the world.

Tourism

Sugar
cane

Acapulco

Corn

Corn

Coffee

Belmopan

BELIZE

GUATEMALA

Teardrop
butterfly fish

Guatemala City

San Salvador

Teguci
al

EL SALVADOR

Coffee

Managua

Swordfish

Clown fish

This distance is the same as 700km
on the ground.

Sea horses

Sperm whale

To the south of the United States, a narrow strip of land containing eight countries links North America with South America. The largest of these is Mexico, a country with a long history and contrasting landscapes. Further south are the seven nations of Central America. Many people in Central America are farmers, who grow food for themselves or work on sugar, coffee or banana plantations. Further east, in the warm Caribbean Sea, lie hundreds of sun-drenched islands. They are famous for their coral reefs and beautiful sandy beaches.

FACT FINDER

▶ Which ancient city in Mexico was built by an American Indian people called the Maya over one thousand years ago? (See square H 8.)

▶ Which shortcut is used by cargo ships to sail between the Atlantic and Pacific Oceans? It is over 80km long and about 30 ships pass through it each day. (See square K 12.)

▶ Which is the only kind of bear to live in Central America? It is named after the white circles around its eyes. (See D 7.)

▶ Which is one of the largest cities in the world, where more people live than in the whole of Australia? (See square E 8.)

Tourism

Reef sharks

ATLANTIC OCEAN

6

Right whale

BAHAMAS

Tropic of Cancer

Cruise ship

7

gar cane

Havana

Beef cattle

CUBA

Tourism

DOMINICAN REPUBLIC

Hummingbird

VIRGIN ISLANDS
(USA & UK)

8

Flamingoes

Tobacco

Coffee

ANGUILLA

San Juan

PUERTO RICO
(USA)

ANTIGUA & BARBUDA

HAITI

Santo Domingo

ST KITTS & NEVIS

GUADELOUPE
(France)

9

Tuna

GREATER

Tourism

Port-au-Prince

A N T I L L E S

JAMAICA

Kingston

DOMINICA

LESSER ANTILLES

MARTINIQUE
(France)

Tourism

HONDURAS

Dolphin

ST LUCIA

10

Sailing

ST VINCENT & THE GRENADINES

BARBADOS

Bananas

C a r i b b e a n   S e a

Anole lizard

Royal gramma fish

GRENADA

11

NICARAGUA

Scuba diving

CURAÇAO
(Netherlands)

TRINIDAD & TOBAGO

Cotton

Panama Canal

Leatherback turtle

Oil

San José

Toucan

Cargo ships

12

offee

Panama City

PANAMA

VENEZUELA

COSTA RICA

COLOMBIA

13

Cargo ship in Panama Canal

South America

The continent of South America stretches from the warm Caribbean Sea to the stormy waters around Cape Horn. South America is warm all year, except in the far south and in the high Andes Mountains. In the north, the great River Amazon flows through tropical rainforest. Further south, there are flat plains where millions of cattle graze. Most South Americans live in cities on the coast. In the country, the farmers grow bananas, coffee beans and corn.

Caribbean Sea

Cargo ships

Royal gramma fish

Tourism
Bananas
Gold

Oil
Oil
Oil

VENEZUELA
Caracas
Oil
Cow tree
River Orinoco
Diamonds
Making clothes
Gold

Emeralds

Cali
COLOMBIA
Bogotá
Coffee
Stilt house

Tapir

Coffee
Oil
Quito
ECUADOR
Bananas
Herring
Coffee
Oil

Rice
Rice
Rice
GUYANA
Georgetown
Angel Falls
Gold

SURINAM
Paramaribo
Gold

Cayenne
FRENCH GUIANA (France)

Crocodile

Equator
Shrimp

Emerald tree boa

Dug-out canoes

River Amazon

Piranha fish

Amazon rainforest

Toucan

Oil

Vampire bat

Sloth

Jaguar

Umbrella bird

Arrow-poison frog

Lake Titicaca

Gold

Copper
Llama
Cotton
Sugar cane

PERU
Lima
Copper

Gold
Sugar cane

BOLIVIA
La Paz
Cotton
Potatoes
Copper
Tin

Gas
Gold
Oil
Cotton
Corn
Cattle ranching

Wheat

Rice
Oranges
Iron
Coffee
Cotton

Cargo ships

Recife

Shrimp

Lobster

Sugar cane
Cotton
Gold
Oil

Tobacco
Gold
Diamonds

Rainforest clearing

Iron
Corn
Brasília

River São Francisco

Tourism

Cotton

Carnival
Rio de Janeiro

BRAZIL

Sperm whale

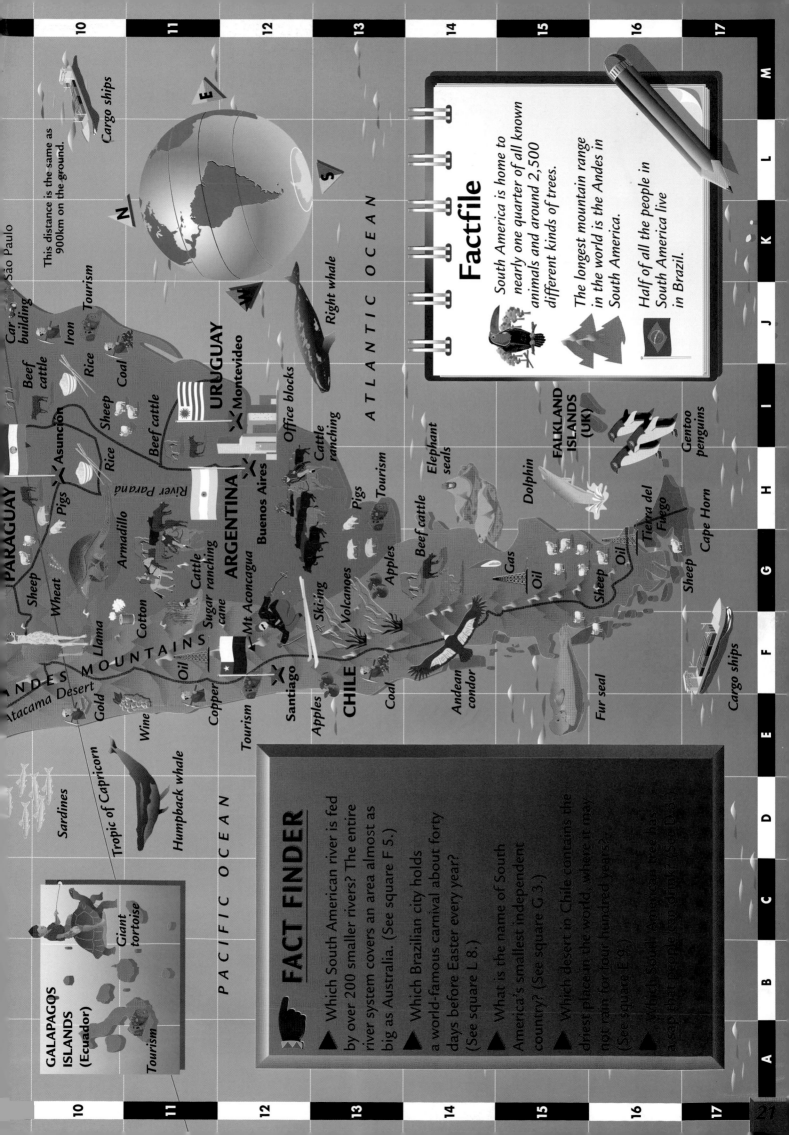

Factfile

South America is home to nearly one quarter of all known animals and around 2,500 different kinds of trees.

The longest mountain range in the world is the Andes in South America.

Half of all the people in South America live in Brazil.

FACT FINDER

▲ Which South American river is fed by over 200 smaller rivers? The entire river system covers an area almost as big as Australia. (See square F 5.)

▲ Which Brazilian city holds a world-famous carnival about forty days before Easter every year? (See square L 8.)

▲ What is the name of South America's smallest independent country? (See square G 3.)

▲ Which desert in Chile contains the driest place in the world, where it may not rain for four hundred years? (See square E 9.)

▲ Which South American tree has a cap that children drink? (See D 5.)

Map labels:

PARAGUAY — Asunción
URUGUAY — Montevideo
ARGENTINA — Buenos Aires
CHILE — Santiago
FALKLAND ISLANDS (UK)
GALAPAGOS ISLANDS (Ecuador)
ANDES MOUNTAINS
Atacama Desert
River Paraná
Mt Aconcagua
Tierra del Fuego
Cape Horn
Tropic of Capricorn

PACIFIC OCEAN
ATLANTIC OCEAN

This distance is the same as 900km on the ground.

N E S W

Products and wildlife: Cargo ships, Car building, São Paulo, Iron, Tourism, Beef cattle, Rice, Coal, Sheep, Rice, Beef cattle, Pigs, Wheat, Sheep, Llama, Armadillo, Cotton, Gold, Wine, Copper, Oil, Sugar cane, Cattle ranching, Tourism, Apples, Coal, Volcanoes, Ski-ing, Apples, Pigs, Tourism, Office blocks, Right whale, Cattle ranching, Beef cattle, Elephant seals, Dolphin, Andean condor, Gas, Oil, Beef cattle, Fur seal, Sheep, Oil, Sheep, Cargo ships, Gentoo penguins, Humpback whale, Sardines, Giant tortoise, Tourism

21

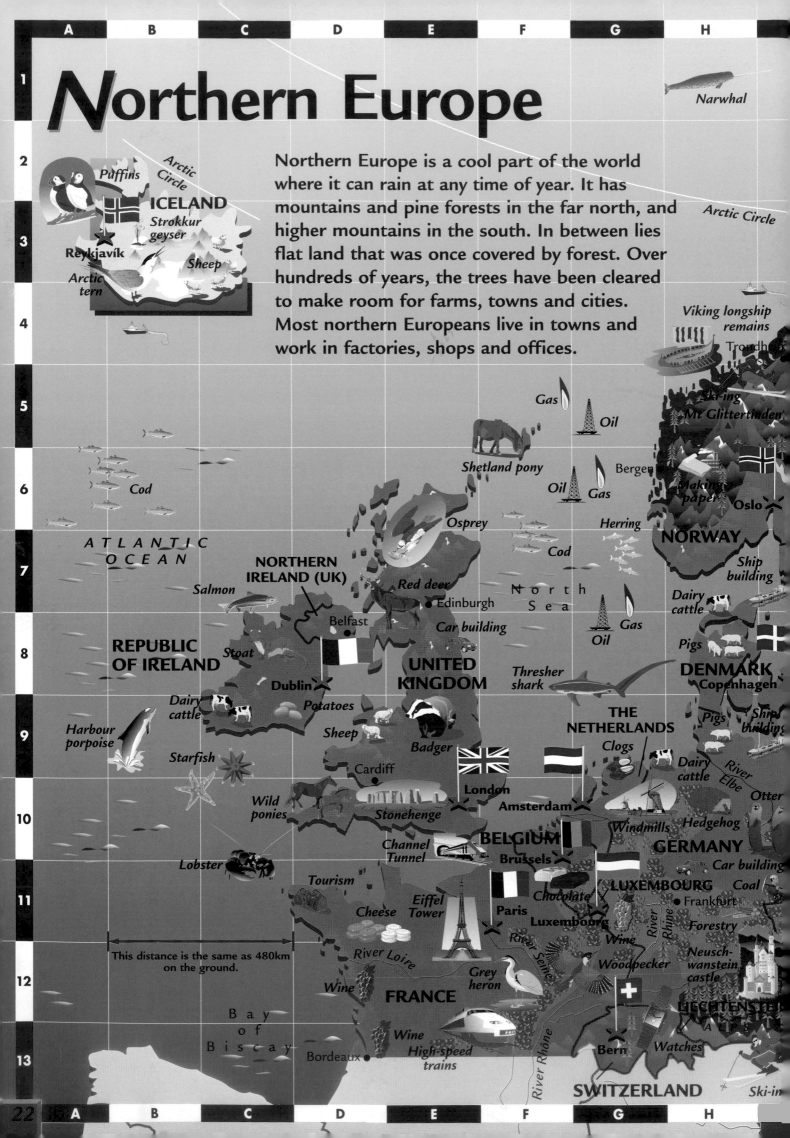

Northern Europe

A B C D E F G H

Narwhal

Northern Europe is a cool part of the world where it can rain at any time of year. It has mountains and pine forests in the far north, and higher mountains in the south. In between lies flat land that was once covered by forest. Over hundreds of years, the trees have been cleared to make room for farms, towns and cities. Most northern Europeans live in towns and work in factories, shops and offices.

Arctic Circle

Puffins

Arctic Circle

ICELAND

Strokkur geyser

Reykjavík

Sheep

Arctic tern

Viking longship remains

Trondheim

Gas

Oil

Ski-ing Mt Glittertinden

Shetland pony

Bergen

Oil *Gas*

Making paper

Oslo

Cod

Osprey

Herring

NORWAY

A T L A N T I C
O C E A N

Cod

N o r t h
S e a

Ship building

Salmon

NORTHERN IRELAND (UK)

Red deer

Edinburgh

Dairy cattle

Gas

Belfast

Car building

Oil

Pigs

REPUBLIC OF IRELAND

Stoat

UNITED KINGDOM

Thresher shark

DENMARK
Copenhagen

Harbour porpoise

Dairy cattle

Dublin

Potatoes

Pigs

Ship building

THE NETHERLANDS

Starfish

Sheep

Badger

Clogs

Dairy cattle

River Elbe

Otter

Cardiff

London

Hedgehog

Wild ponies

Stonehenge

Amsterdam

Windmills

GERMANY

BELGIUM

Car building

Lobster

Channel Tunnel

Brussels

Chocolate

LUXEMBOURG *Coal*

Tourism

Cheese

Eiffel Tower

Paris

Frankfurt

Luxembourg

Wine

Forestry

This distance is the same as 480km on the ground.

Wine

River Loire

Grey heron

Woodpecker

Neuschwanstein castle

FRANCE

LIECHTENSTEIN

B a y
o f
B i s c a y

Wine
High-speed trains

Bern

Watches

Bordeaux

River Rhône

SWITZERLAND

Ski-ing

22

Norwegian
Sea

KJØLEN MOUNTAINS

Lapland

Reindeer

Sami people

Iron

Cross-country ski-ing

Forestry

Forestry

Making
paper

Forestry

FINLAND

SWEDEN

Making paper

Salmon

Lynx

Herring

Fox

Helsinki

Stockholm

Ice
breakers

Tallinn

Pigs

Car building

ESTONIA

Göteborg

Dairy
cattle

Building
trains

Riga

LATVIA

Baltic
Sea

RUSSIA

LITHUANIA

Malmö

Vilnius

Ship building

Kaliningrad
(Russia)

BELARUS

ship building

Potatoes

Dairy cattle

Red squirrel

Chaffinch

erlin

Wild boar

Warsaw

POLAND

Wolf

Coal

UKRAINE

Prague

Chamois

CZECH
REPUBLIC

SLOVAKIA

Vienna

Danube

Bratislava

Parliament
building

AUSTRIA

Peregrine
falcon

ROMANIA

Budapest

HUNGARY

Wild horses

FACT FINDER

▶ Which tunnel in northern Europe is nearly 50km long and allows 400 trains to pass along it in each direction every day? (See square E 10.)

▶ In which country could you see a longship on display, which was built by the Viking people hundreds of years ago? (See square H 4.)

▶ Which famous European tower is 320m high and has 1,652 steps that take you to the top? (See square E 11.)

▶ Which stone monument in England was built around 3,500 years ago, but nobody knows what it was used for? (See square E 10.)

N

W   E

S

Factfile

There are twice as many pigs in Denmark as people. Two out of three pigs are exported as Danish bacon.

France is visited by more tourists each year than any other country in the world.

Finland produces enough paper to make 5 million comics every day.

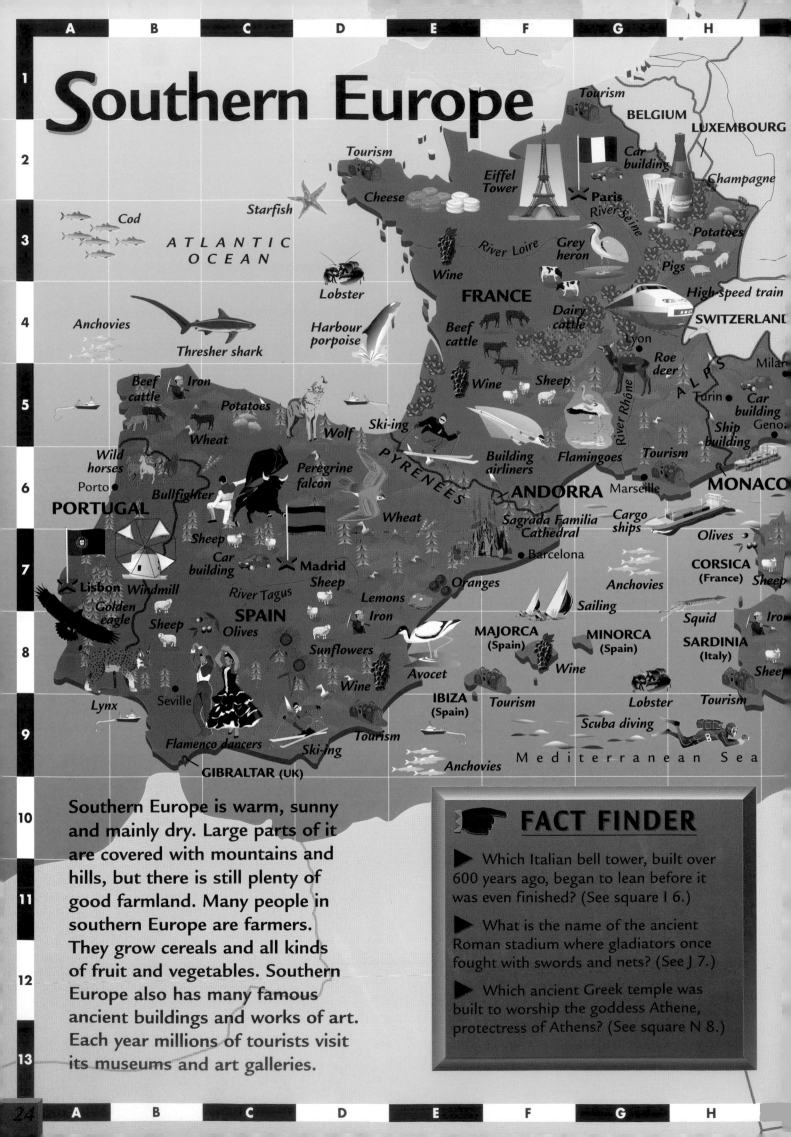

Southern Europe

Southern Europe is warm, sunny and mainly dry. Large parts of it are covered with mountains and hills, but there is still plenty of good farmland. Many people in southern Europe are farmers. They grow cereals and all kinds of fruit and vegetables. Southern Europe also has many famous ancient buildings and works of art. Each year millions of tourists visit its museums and art galleries.

FACT FINDER

► Which Italian bell tower, built over 600 years ago, began to lean before it was even finished? (See square I 6.)

► What is the name of the ancient Roman stadium where gladiators once fought with swords and nets? (See J 7.)

► Which ancient Greek temple was built to worship the goddess Athene, protectress of Athens? (See square N 8.)

Factfile

Mount Etna in Sicily is the largest volcano in Europe. It last erupted in 1995.

Spain produces more olive oil than any other country. Each year it produces enough olive oil to fill 160 Olympic-sized swimming pools.

This distance is the same as 400km on the ground.

Russia and its neighbours

A B C D E F G H

1

2

3 EUROPE · SWEDEN · ARCTIC OCEAN · Ice breakers

4 Kaliningrad (Russia) · St Petersburg · Murmansk · Russian dolls · Ice breakers · Badger · Archangel · Forestry · Snowy owl

5 Forestry · Potatoes · Gas · Minsk · BELARUS · Russian dolls · Forestry · Bolshoi Ballet · Gas · Coal · Winter camp of Nentsy people · Gas

6 Moscow · St Basil's Cathedral · Nizhniy Novgorod · Car building · Oil · Wolf · Chisinau · Sugar beet · Kiev · Potatoes · River Ob · Oil

7 MOLDOVA · UKRAINE · Corn · Coal · River Don · Sugar beet · Tractor building · Barley · R U S · Tourism · River Volga · Oil · Gold · Hamster · Black Sea · Wine · Volgograd · Iron · Wheat · S t e p p e

8 TURKEY · GEORGIA · Wheat · Pigs · Crane · Baikonur Space Centre · Beef cattle · Coa · Mt Elbrus · Pelican · KAZAKHSTAN

9 Tbilisi · Sturgeon · Oil · Iron · Copper · River Irtysh · ARMENIA · Yerevan · Gymnastics · Sunflowers · AZERBAIJAN · Caspian Sea · Aral Sea

10 Cotton · Baku · Kara Kum Desert · Cotton · UZBEKISTAN · Tobacco · Gas · Carpet weaving · Gas · Cotton · Bishkek · Alma-Ata · Tashkent · KYRGYZSTA

11 Ashgabat · River Amu Darya · Dushanbe · Wild horses · Cotton · TAJIKISTAN · TURKMENISTAN · Oil

FACT FINDER

▶ Which space centre launched the world's first astronaut, Yuri Gagarin, into space in 1961? (See square G 8.)

▶ Which Russian railway line is the longest railway line in the world? It takes just over eight days to travel along it from one end to the other. (See J 8.)

12 A S I A

13 This distance is the same as 1,100km on the ground.

A B C D E F G H

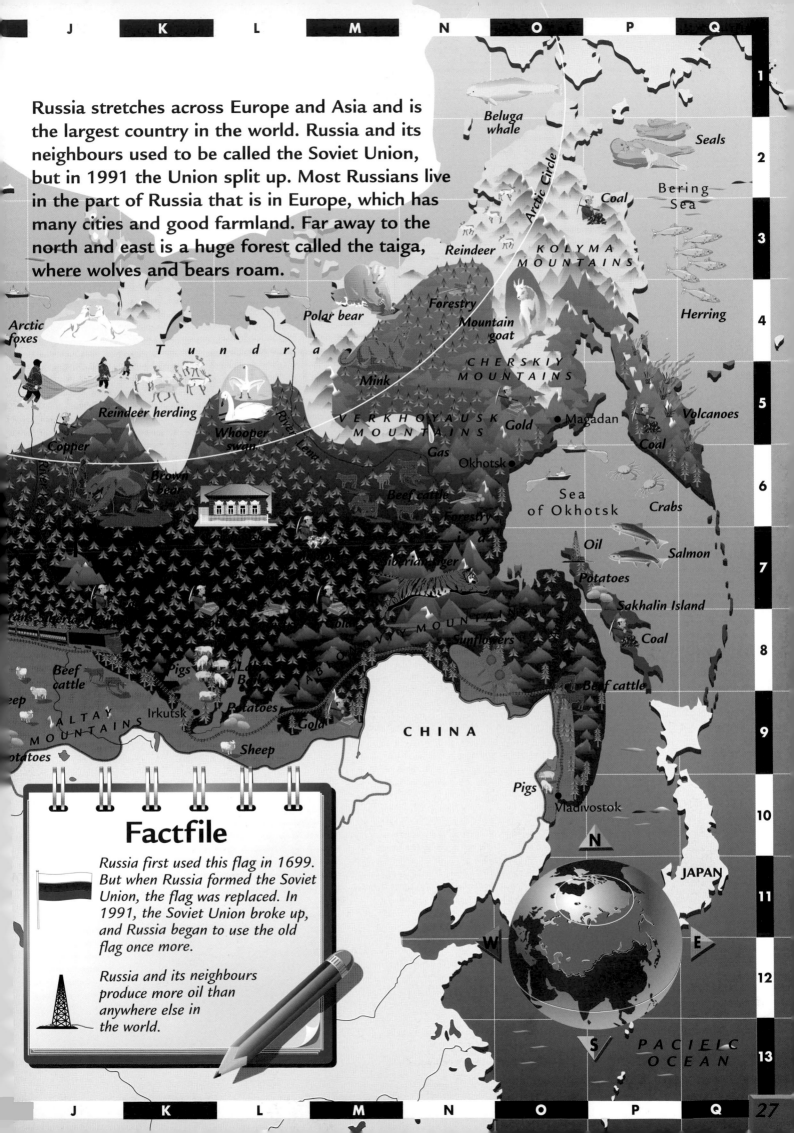

Russia stretches across Europe and Asia and is the largest country in the world. Russia and its neighbours used to be called the Soviet Union, but in 1991 the Union split up. Most Russians live in the part of Russia that is in Europe, which has many cities and good farmland. Far away to the north and east is a huge forest called the taiga, where wolves and bears roam.

Factfile

Russia first used this flag in 1699. But when Russia formed the Soviet Union, the flag was replaced. In 1991, the Soviet Union broke up, and Russia began to use the old flag once more.

Russia and its neighbours produce more oil than anywhere else in the world.

Map labels: Beluga whale, Seals, Bering Sea, Coal, Herring, Reindeer, KOLYMA MOUNTAINS, Arctic Circle, Polar bear, Forestry, Mountain goat, Arctic foxes, Tundra, Mink, CHERSKIY MOUNTAINS, Volcanoes, Reindeer herding, Whooper swan, River Lena, VERKHOYANSK MOUNTAINS, Gold, Magadan, Coal, Copper, Gas, Okhotsk, Brown bear, Beef cattle, Sea of Okhotsk, Crabs, Forestry, Oil, Salmon, Siberian tiger, Potatoes, Sakhalin Island, Sunflowers, Coal, Beef cattle, Beef cattle, Pigs, ALTAY MOUNTAINS, Irkutsk, Potatoes, Gold, CHINA, Sheep, Pigs, Vladivostok, JAPAN, PACIFIC OCEAN

27

The Middle East

The south-west corner of Asia is called the Middle East. Here, thousands of years ago, people first became farmers, then settled close together in towns. Much of the land in the Middle East is hot, dry desert, which can be hard to farm.

Fifty years ago, people found oil under the desert. They used the money they made from the oil to build huge watering systems, so they could grow crops more easily in the poor soil. They also built large cities.

Factfile

Over 5,000 years ago, the first cities in the world grew up in the Middle East, along the Tigris and Euphrates Rivers.

Three of the world's major religions began in the Middle East. They are Islam, Judaism and Christianity.

The Middle East makes some of the world's most expensive hand-made carpets. Carpet-makers weave and knot wool to make different patterns which can tell you the area the carpet comes from.

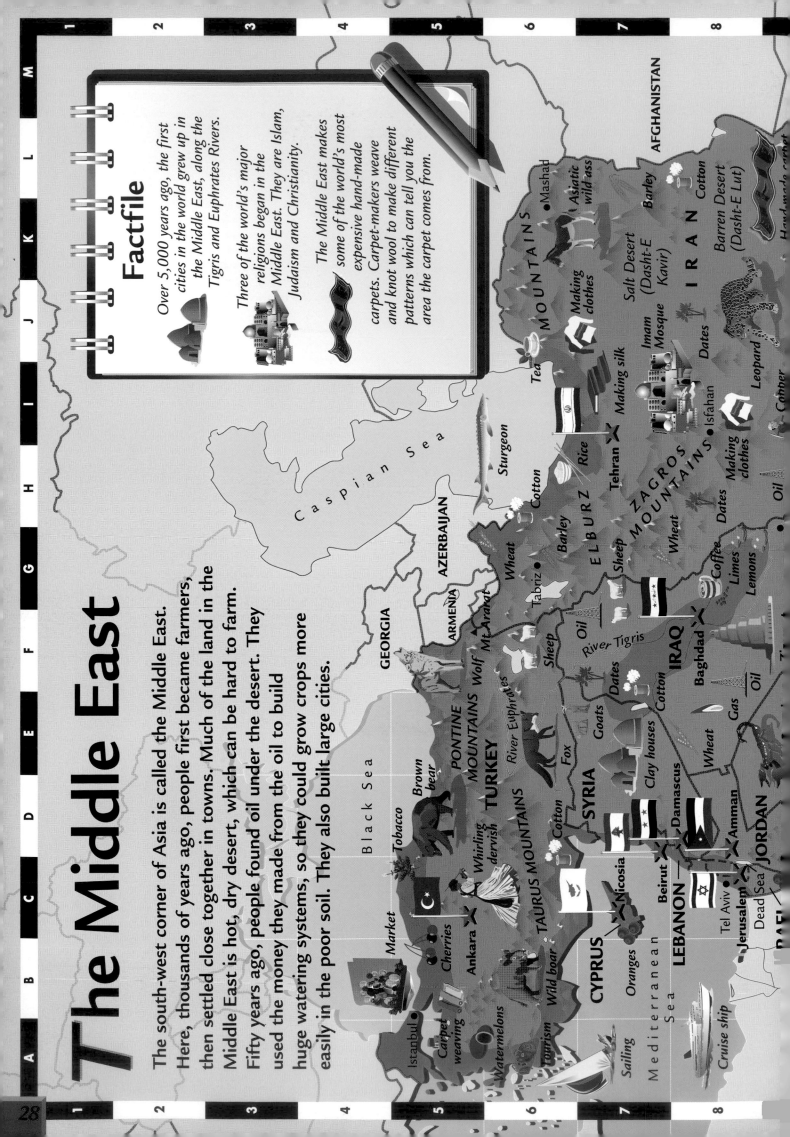

AFGHANISTAN

Mashad

Asiatic wild ass

Barley

Making clothes

Salt Desert (Dasht-E Kavir)

IRAN

Cotton

Barren Desert (Dasht-E Lut)

Copper

Leopard

Dates

Making silk

Imam Mosque

Isfahan

Making clothes

Tea

MOUNTAINS

Rice

Tehran

ZAGROS MOUNTAINS

Dates

Wheat

Oil

Sturgeon

Cotton

Caspian Sea

Barley

ELBURZ MOUNTAINS

Sheep

Coffee

Limes

Lemons

Wheat

AZERBAIJAN

Wheat

Tabriz

Oil

River Tigris

Dates

IRAQ

Baghdad

Gas

Oil

ARMENIA

Mt Ararat

Sheep

Wolf

Fox

Goats

Dates

Cotton

Clay houses

Wheat

GEORGIA

PONTINE MOUNTAINS

River Euphrates

SYRIA

Damascus

Black Sea

Brown bear

Tobacco

Market

TURKEY

TAURUS MOUNTAINS

Cotton

Amman

Whirling dervish

Wild boar

Cherries

Ankara

Beirut

LEBANON

JORDAN

Watermelons

Tourism

CYPRUS

Oranges

Nicosia

Tel Aviv

Jerusalem

Dead Sea

Istanbul

Carpet weaving

Sailing

Mediterranean Sea

Cruise ship

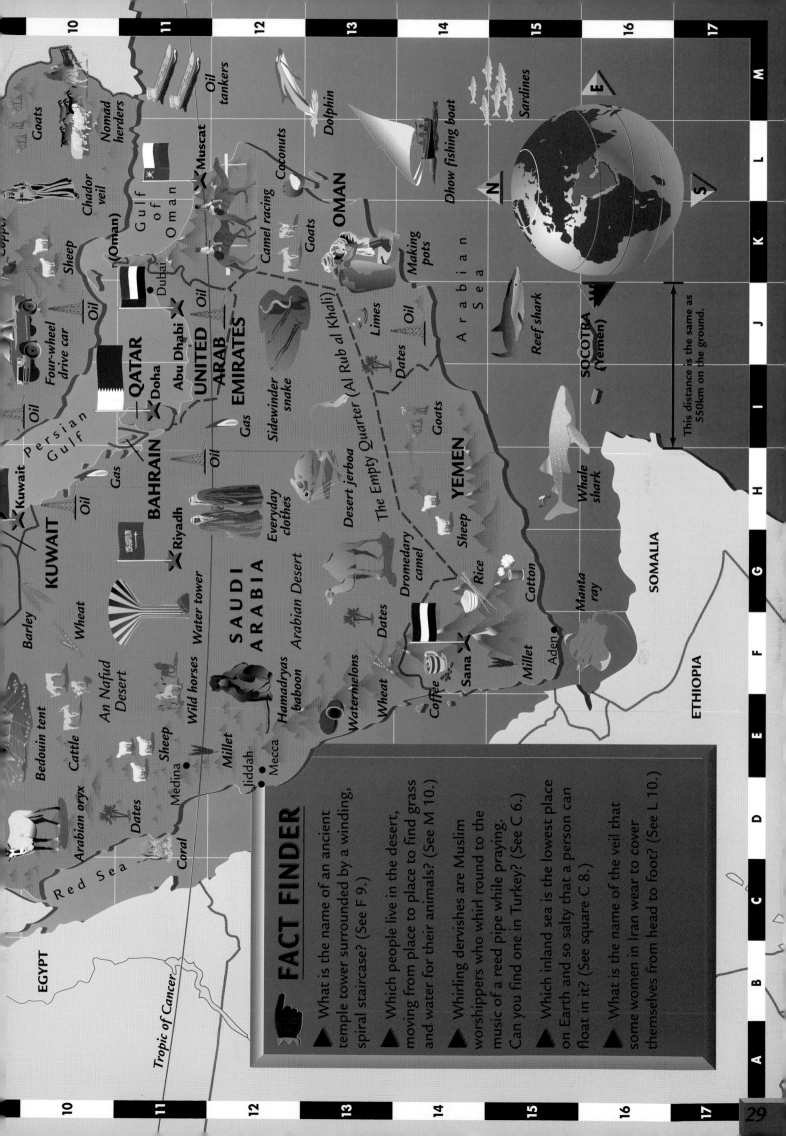

FACT FINDER

▲ What is the name of an ancient temple tower surrounded by a winding, spiral staircase? (See F 9.)

▲ Which people live in the desert, moving from place to place to find grass and water for their animals? (See M 10.)

▲ Whirling dervishes are Muslim worshippers who whirl round to the music of a reed pipe while praying. Can you find one in Turkey? (See C 6.)

▲ Which inland sea is the lowest place on Earth and so salty that a person can float in it? (See square C 8.)

▲ What is the name of the veil that some women in Iran wear to cover themselves from head to foot? (See L 10.)

Northern Africa

Mediterranean Sea

ATLANTIC OCEAN

MADEIRA (Portugal)

Wine

Barley

Oran

Algiers

Tunis

Tourism

Casablanca

Rabat

Wine

Wheat

TUNISIA

Wine

Marrakech

MOROCCO

ATLAS MOUNTAINS

Tripoli

Souk market

Scorpion

Swallowtail butterfly

Olives

Oil

Tourism

CANARY ISLANDS (Spain)

El Aaiún

ALGERIA

Wheat

Peanut

LIBYA

Tropic of Cancer

WESTERN SAHARA

Goats

Tuareg caravan

Tuareg horseman

Oil

Dates

Sheep

Sahara Desert

AHAGGAR MOUNTAINS

Desert lizard

Salt

Iron

Dromedary camel

MAURITANIA

Houses of the Dogon people

Secretary bird

Nouakchott

MALI

NIGER

Iron

Copper

Dakar

Iron

Cattle

Djénné Mosque

Cattle

Cotton

Ostrich

SENEGAL

Cotton

Grain store

Salt

Banjul

Lion

Grain store

Lake Chad

GAMBIA

Bissau

BURKINA FASO

Niamey

Bamako

Ouagadougou

N'Djamen

GUINEA-BISSAU

Coffee

Gold

Tin

Hippopotamus

Conakry

GUINEA

Coffee

Cotton

BENIN

Diamonds

Cotton

River Niger

Abuja

Cott

Freetown

Cotton

GHANA

NIGERIA

SIERRA LEONE

IVORY COAST

Lake Volta

TOGO

Monrovia

Iron

Forestry

Lagos

LIBERIA

Abidjan

Accra

Lomé

Porto-Novo

Oil

CAMEROON

CENTR AFRICA REPUB

Cargo ships

Oil

SÃO TOMÉ & PRÍNCIPE

CONG

GABON

ZAIR

Many different peoples live in northern Africa. Most of them herd animals or farm the land. Northern Africa is hot all over, but not all of it is dry desert. The north coast has enough rain to grow fruit. Its large cities have busy markets and beautiful Muslim mosques. Tropical forests near the equator bring rain to the farmers' crops. But further east, the soil is poor and dry.

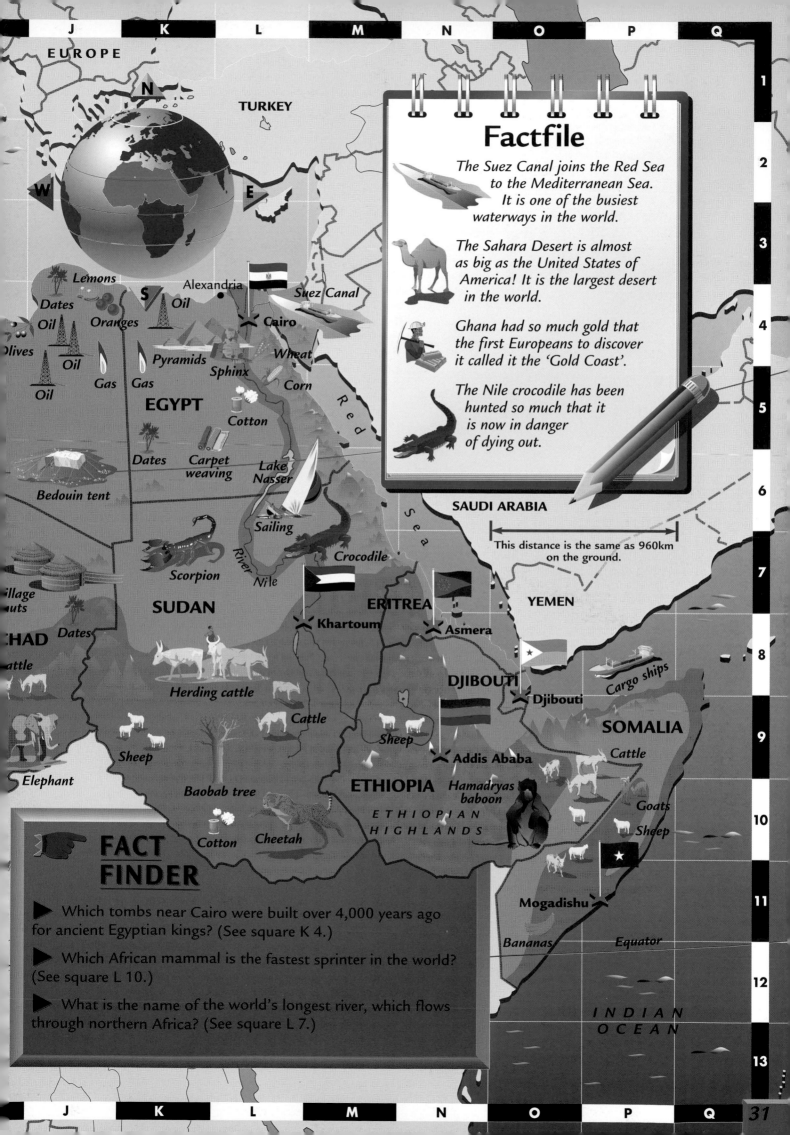

EUROPE

TURKEY

N

W   E

S

Factfile

The Suez Canal joins the Red Sea to the Mediterranean Sea. It is one of the busiest waterways in the world.

The Sahara Desert is almost as big as the United States of America! It is the largest desert in the world.

Ghana had so much gold that the first Europeans to discover it called it the 'Gold Coast'.

The Nile crocodile has been hunted so much that it is now in danger of dying out.

Lemons

Dates

Oil   Oranges

Olives   Oil

Oil   Gas   Gas

Oil

Alexandria

Oil

Suez Canal

Cairo

Pyramids

Sphinx

Wheat

Corn

EGYPT

Cotton

Dates   Carpet weaving

Lake Nasser

Bedouin tent

Sailing

River Nile

Scorpion

Crocodile

Red Sea

SAUDI ARABIA

This distance is the same as 960km on the ground.

SUDAN

Khartoum

ERITREA

Asmera

YEMEN

Village huts

CHAD

Dates

attle

Herding cattle

Cattle

DJIBOUTI

Djibouti

Cargo ships

SOMALIA

Sheep

Sheep

Addis Ababa

Cattle

Elephant

ETHIOPIA

Hamadryas baboon

E T H I O P I A N
H I G H L A N D S

Goats

Sheep

Baobab tree

Cotton   Cheetah

Mogadishu

Bananas   Equator

I N D I A N
O C E A N

FACT FINDER

▶ Which tombs near Cairo were built over 4,000 years ago for ancient Egyptian kings? (See square K 4.)

▶ Which African mammal is the fastest sprinter in the world? (See square L 10.)

▶ What is the name of the world's longest river, which flows through northern Africa? (See square L 7.)

Southern Africa

Southern Africa is a vast land of grasslands, rainforests, mountains and deserts. The plains of Kenya and Tanzania are famous for their huge herds of animals. Further west, in the rainforests, there are gorillas, monkeys and tropical birds. Many different peoples live in Africa. Most of them farm in small villages, but the cities are growing. Many countries mine copper and gold. Some mine diamonds too.

Factfile

Southern Africa is home to the black rhino and the mountain gorilla, two of the world's most endangered animals.

Southern Africa has large areas of rainforest. Altogether, nearly one quarter of the world's forests grow in southern Africa.

Three-quarters of the world's diamonds are mined in southern Africa.

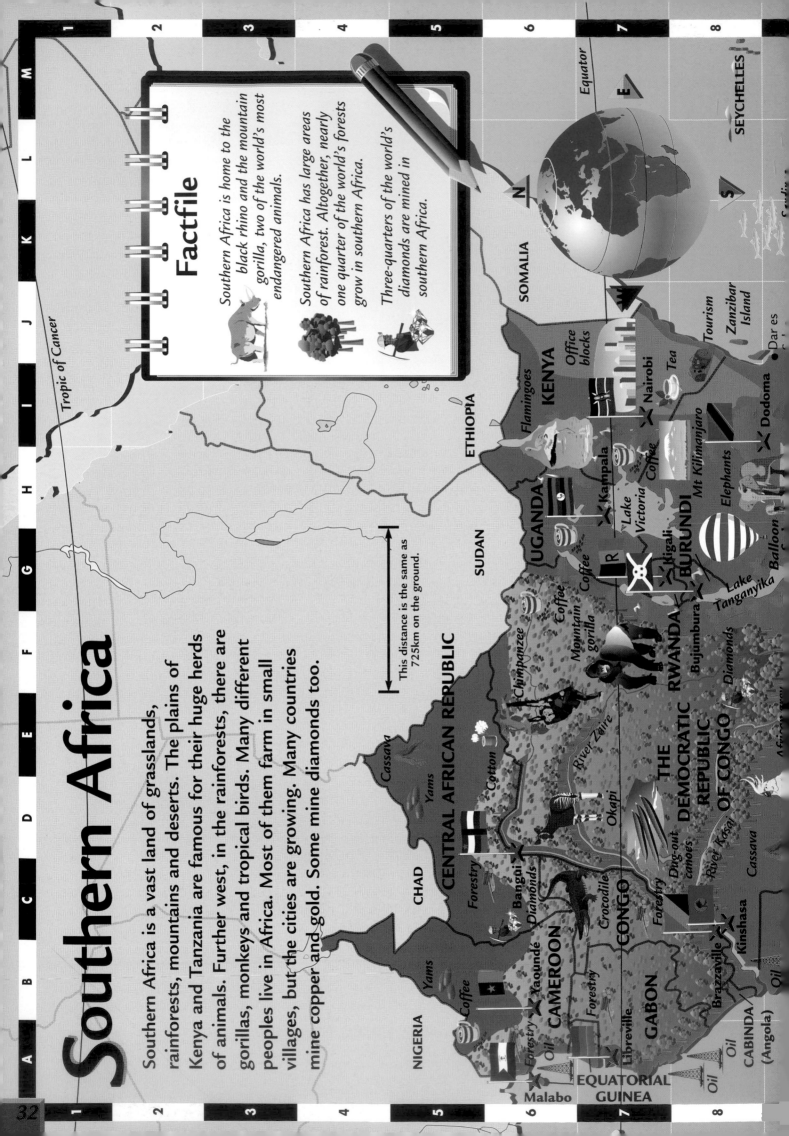

Tropic of Cancer

Equator

This distance is the same as 725km on the ground.

N

E

W

S

SEYCHELLES

SOMALIA

Office blocks

KENYA

Nairobi

Tea

Coffee

Mt Kilimanjaro

Elephants

Tourism

Zanzibar Island

Dar es

Dodoma

Balloon

Lake Tanganyika

ETHIOPIA

Flamingoes

Lake Victoria

Kampala

UGANDA

Coffee

Kigali

RWANDA

BURUNDI

Bujumbura

SUDAN

Coffee

Mountain gorilla

R

Diamonds

Chimpanzee

THE DEMOCRATIC REPUBLIC OF CONGO

CENTRAL AFRICAN REPUBLIC

CHAD

Cassava

Yams

Cotton

River Zaire

Okapi

River Kasai

Cassava

Dug-out canoes

Bangui

Diamonds

Forestry

NIGERIA

Yams

Coffee

Yaoundé

Forestry

Oil

CAMEROON

Forestry

Forestry

Crocodile

Forestry

CONGO

Brazzaville

Kinshasa

Libreville

GABON

Malabo

EQUATORIAL GUINEA

Oil

Oil

Oil

CABINDA (Angola)

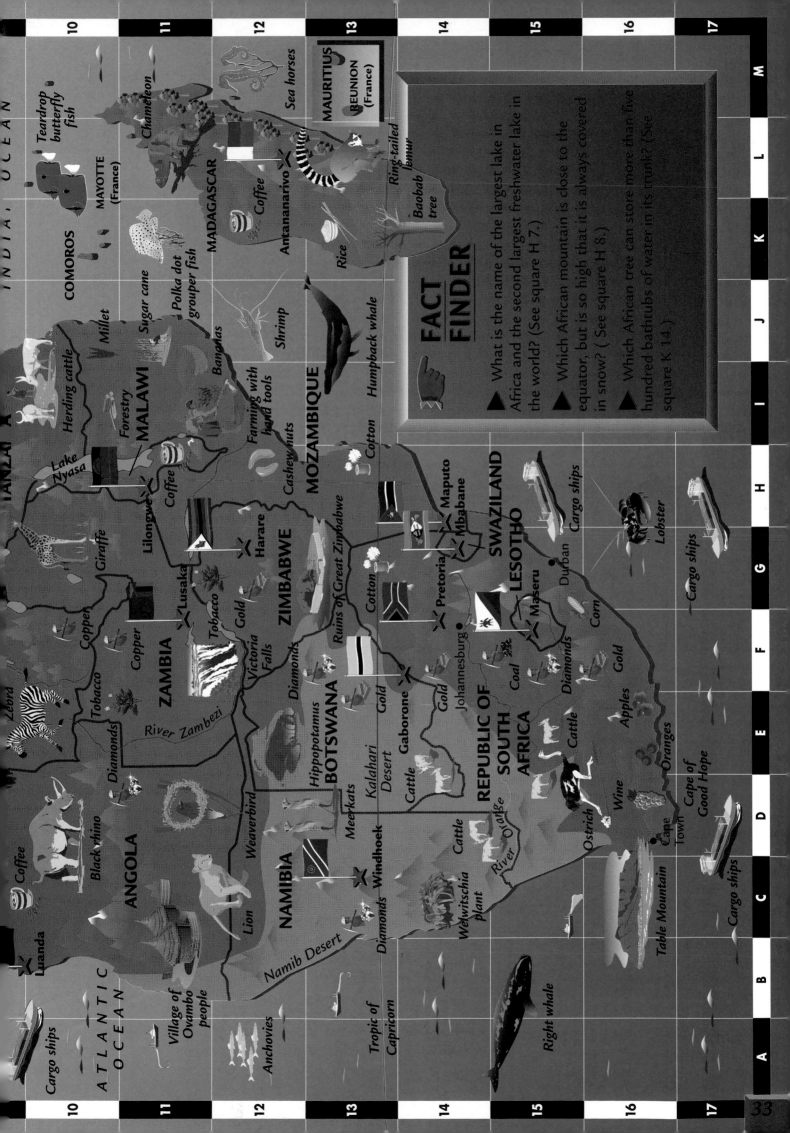

INDIAN OCEAN

ATLANTIC OCEAN

FACT FINDER

▲ What is the name of the largest lake in Africa and the second largest freshwater lake in the world? (See square H 7.)

▲ Which African mountain is close to the equator, but is so high that it is always covered in snow? (See square H 8.)

▲ Which African tree can store more than five hundred bathtubs of water in its trunk? (See square K 14.)

MAYOTTE (France)

Teardrop butterfly fish

Chameleon

Sea horses

MAURITIUS

REUNION (France)

MADAGASCAR

Coffee

Antananarivo

Rice

Ring-tailed lemur

Baobab tree

COMOROS

Sugar cane

Polka dot grouper fish

Bananas

Millet

Herding cattle

Forestry

MALAWI

Lilongwe

Coffee

Farming with hand tools

Cashew nuts

Shrimp

MOZAMBIQUE

Humpback whale

Cotton

Lake Nyasa

TANZANIA

Zebra

Giraffe

Copper

Tobacco

Coffee

ZAMBIA

Lusaka

Copper

Copper

Tobacco

Gold

Victoria Falls

Tobacco

ZIMBABWE

Harare

Ruins of Great Zimbabwe

Diamonds

River Zambezi

Diamonds

Black rhino

Coffee

Luanda

ANGOLA

Lion

Village of Ovambo people

Weaverbird

NAMIBIA

Windhoek

Diamonds

Namib Desert

Tropic of Capricorn

Anchovies

Welwitschia plant

Cattle

River Orange

Cattle

Meerkats

Kalahari Desert

BOTSWANA

Gaborone

Cattle

Hippopotamus

Cotton

Gold

Maputo

Mbabane

SWAZILAND

LESOTHO

Maseru

Pretoria

Gold

Johannesburg

Coal

Diamonds

Corn

Cargo ships

Durban

Lobster

Cargo ships

REPUBLIC OF SOUTH AFRICA

Gold

Cattle

Diamonds

Gold

Apples

Wine

Oranges

Ostrich

Cape Town

Cape of Good Hope

Table Mountain

Cargo ships

Right whale

33

Southern Asia

Southern Asia stretches from the Himalayan Mountains in the north of India to the island of Sri Lanka in the south. The weather is mostly hot and dry, although for several months of the year there are heavy rains. More than a billion people live in southern Asia. Most people live in villages and farm the land, but many are beginning to move to the cities. The cities are a mixture of old and new, with modern buildings next to ancient temples and palaces. The busy streets are packed with cars, trucks and lorries, but also with bullock carts and elephants.

FACT FINDER

▲ Which white marble temple, decorated with precious stones, was built in the 17th century by an Indian emperor as a burial place for his wife? (See square G 8.)

▲ In India, which animal is used to help people with heavy work such as moving timber? (See square F 11.)

▲ What are Pakistan, Afghanistan and India all famous for weaving? (See squares C 6, C 9 and F 7.)

▲ In India, which three-wheeled vehicle that looks a little like a bicycle is often used to carry people from one place to another? (See square I 10.)

CHINA

TURKMENISTAN

UZBEKISTAN

TAJIKISTAN

AFGHANISTAN

Bactrian camel

Milking goats

Cotton

Wheat

Cattle

Blue Mosque

Carpet weaving

Kabul

Rubies

Peaches

River Helmand

Goats

Quetta

PAKISTAN

Cotton

Wheat

River Indus

Thar

Cobra

Wheat

Shah Faisal Mosque

Sugar cane

Islamabad

Lahore

Making

Cattle

Wheat

Sugar cane

Goats

Carpet weaving

New Delhi

Taj Mahal

KARAKORAM RANGE

Snow leopard

Yak

Mountain peaks

HIMALAYAN MOUNTAINS

Mt Everest

NEPAL

Kathmandu

Sugar cane

BHUTAN

Thimphu

Tea

River Brahmaputra

Indian rhino

Buddhist monk

Tea

Oil

Rice

Factfile

More films are made in southern Asia than anywhere else in the world. India makes over 800 films a year.

The mountains of southern Asia are home to the snow leopard, one of the world's most endangered animals.

Southern Asia is the world's largest producer of tea.

Eastern Asia

Eastern Asia is made up of China, Mongolia, Japan, North and South Korea, Taiwan and Hong Kong. It is a vast land with mountains and deserts in the north and west. Most people live further east, where there is more rain and good farmland. China is a huge country. Many people are farmers and live in the countryside. In Japan, most people live in cities. They work in factories and offices.

RUSSIA

This distance is the same as 450km on the ground.

Goats

Red deer

ALTAI MOUNTAINS

TIEN SHAN MOUNTAINS

Wolf

Copper

Yurt

Ulan Bator

Coal

MONG

Oil

Cotton

Bactrian camel

Gob

Rice

Iron

Goats

Wheat

Sand grouse

Sheep

Wild horses

Cotton

Wild horses

Cotton

Sheep

Takla Makan Desert

Oil

Cotton

Sheep

Great Wall of China

PAKISTAN

Vulture

Gas

K2 (Mt Godwin Austen)

Tai Chi exercises

Calligraphy

Wild boar

Salt mining

TIBET

Snow leopard

CHINA

INDIA

Yak

Cattle

Goats

Sheep

HIMALAYAN MOUNTAINS

Pigs

Chengd

Mountain peaks

Potala Palace

Buddhist monk

▲ Mt Everest

Great Buddha

BHUTAN

INDIA

N

Stone forest

MYANMAR

W

E

Tea

LAOS

S

THAILAND

FACT FINDER

▶ Which ancient exercises do many Chinese people perform every morning to keep themselves healthy? (See E 7).

▶ Which wall is over 6,400km long and was built over 500 years ago to protect China from northern invaders? (See square H 6).

▶ What is the name of the tent-like dwelling that Mongolian live in to protect themselves from the heat and cold? (See square G 3).

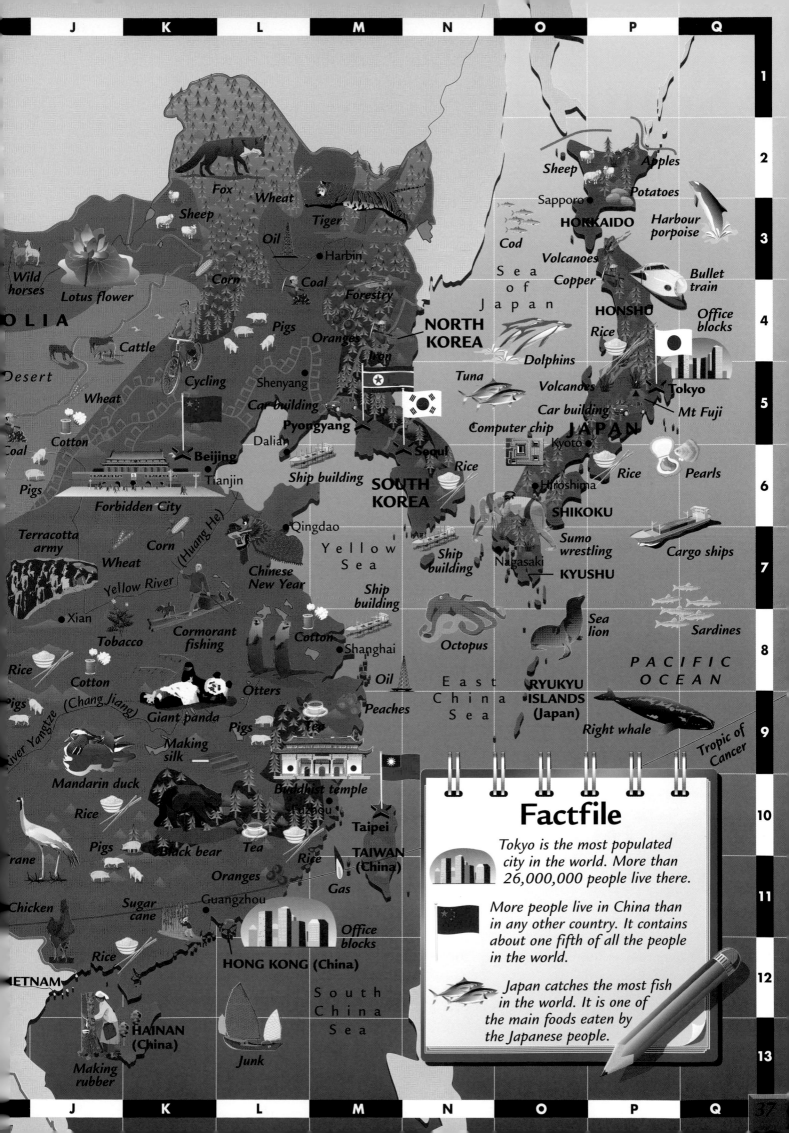

1

Sheep
Apples
Sapporo
Potatoes

2

HOKKAIDO
Harbour
porpoise
Cod
Volcanoes

S e a
o f
Copper

3

J a p a n
HONSHU
Bullet
train

NORTH
KOREA
Rice
Office
blocks

4

Dolphins
Volcanoes
Tokyo

Tuna
Car building
Mt Fuji

5

Fox
Wheat
Tiger
Computer chip
JAPAN
Kyoto

Sheep
Oil
Harbin
Coal
Forestry
Pyongyang
Seoul
SOUTH
KOREA
Rice
Hiroshima
Rice
Pearls

6

Corn
Oranges
Iron
Shenyang
Car building
Dalian
Ship building
SHIKOKU

Wild
horses
Lotus flower

OLIA
Cattle
Desert
Wheat
Cycling
Beijing
Tianjin

Pigs
Sumo
wrestling

7

Coal
Cotton
Forbidden City
Qingdao
Y e l l o w
S e a
Ship
building
KYUSHU
Nagasaki
Cargo ships

Pigs

Terracotta
army
Corn
(Huang He)
Ship
building
Ship
building

8

Wheat
Chinese
New Year
Octopus
Sea
lion
Sardines

Yellow River
Xian
Cotton
Shanghai

Rice
Tobacco
Cormorant
fishing
Oil
PACIFIC
OCEAN

Cotton
Otters
E a s t
C h i n a
S e a
RYUKYU
ISLANDS
(Japan)

9

Pigs
(Chang Jiang)
Giant panda
Peaches
Right whale
Tropic of
Cancer

River Yangtze
Pigs
Tea

Mandarin duck
Making
silk

10

Rice
Buddhist temple
Fuzou

crane
Pigs
Black bear
Tea
Taipei

Factfile

Tokyo is the most populated
city in the world. More than
26,000,000 people live there.

Chicken
Oranges
Rice
TAIWAN
(China)

11

Sugar
cane
Guangzhou
Gas

Rice
Office
blocks

More people live in China than
in any other country. It contains
about one fifth of all the people
in the world.

12

HONG KONG (China)

VIETNAM
S o u t h
C h i n a
S e a

Japan catches the most fish
in the world. It is one of
the main foods eaten by
the Japanese people.

13

HAINAN
(China)
Junk

Making
rubber

South-east Asia

South-east Asia is made up of a narrow strip of land and thousands of small islands. The area has high mountains, tropical forests and river valleys. The weather is hot and wet all year round. Many of the people are farmers, who grow rice and corn for food, and rubber and coffee to sell. But the cities are growing, and more people are finding work in factories and offices.

Factfile

Rubber is made from the sap of the rubber tree. South-east Asia produces over three-quarters of the world's rubber.

There are more active volcanoes in south-east Asia than in any other area of the world. The ash left behind from volcanic eruptions helps to make the soil good for farming.

The country of Indonesia is made up of over 13,000 islands. It is the biggest chain of islands in the world and has the world's fourth largest population.

This distance is the same as 800km on the ground.

Bicycle rickshaw

Coconuts
MINDANAO

N E S

NORTH

PACIFIC

OCEAN

Outrigger fishing boat

Equator

Tuna

Bird of paradise

Coconuts

Sponge

Coconuts

Gas Oil

Indonesia

PAPUA NEW

MALUKU

Bananas

Port Moresby

Shrimp

Cloves

Tree kangaroo

Echidna

SULAWESI

Flying lizard

Crab

Humpback whale

Coffee

N E S I A

Manta ray

Komodo dragon

FLORES

TIMOR

BALI

SUMBA

Shrimp

Tourism

N

E

AUSTRALIA

S

Dolphins

Tropic of Capricorn

Australia, New Zealand
and the Pacific Islands

The Pacific Ocean is dotted with thousands of islands. Many people live in villages and grow crops or hunt for fish. Australia is an island too, but it is so big that it is a continent. Most Australians live in cities or farm land near the coast. A lot of Australia is hot and dry, but it has mountains and rainforests too. It also has animals and plants that are not found anywhere else.

Darwin

Shrimp

Manta ray

Crocodile

Beef cattle

Cattle ranching

Road train

Beef cattle

NORTHERN TERRITORY

Cave paintings

Tanami Desert

Boomerang

Diamonds

AUSTRALIA

Beef cattle

Baobab tree

Alice Springs

INDIAN OCEAN

Iron

Water hole

Tiger snake

Uluru (Ayers Rock)

Flying Doctor service

Tropic of Capricorn

Reef sharks

Emu

Sheep

Camels

Dingoes

SOUTH AUSTRALIA

Lake Eyr

Sailing

WESTERN AUSTRALIA

Great Victoria Desert

Opals

Coober Pedy

Echidna

Gold

Budgerigar

Wombat

Orang

Perth

Wave Rock

Koala

Adelaid

Wine

Lobster

Dolphin

FACT FINDER

▶ Which lake in southern Australia is dry for most of the year and covered by a crust of salt nearly four metres thick? (See square H 8.)

▶ Which mammal has a furry body and feeds milk to its young, but has a duck's bill and hatches its young from eggs? This mammal is only found in Australia. (See square J 9.)

▶ Many of Australia's rocks are very old. Can you find one that is shaped like a wave and is over 3,000 million years old? (See square D 9.)

Factfile

The Great Barrier Reef off the east coast of Australia is the biggest coral reef in the world.

Nearly half of the world's 3,000 languages are spoken by people in the Pacific Islands.

Australia is the world's flattest continent.

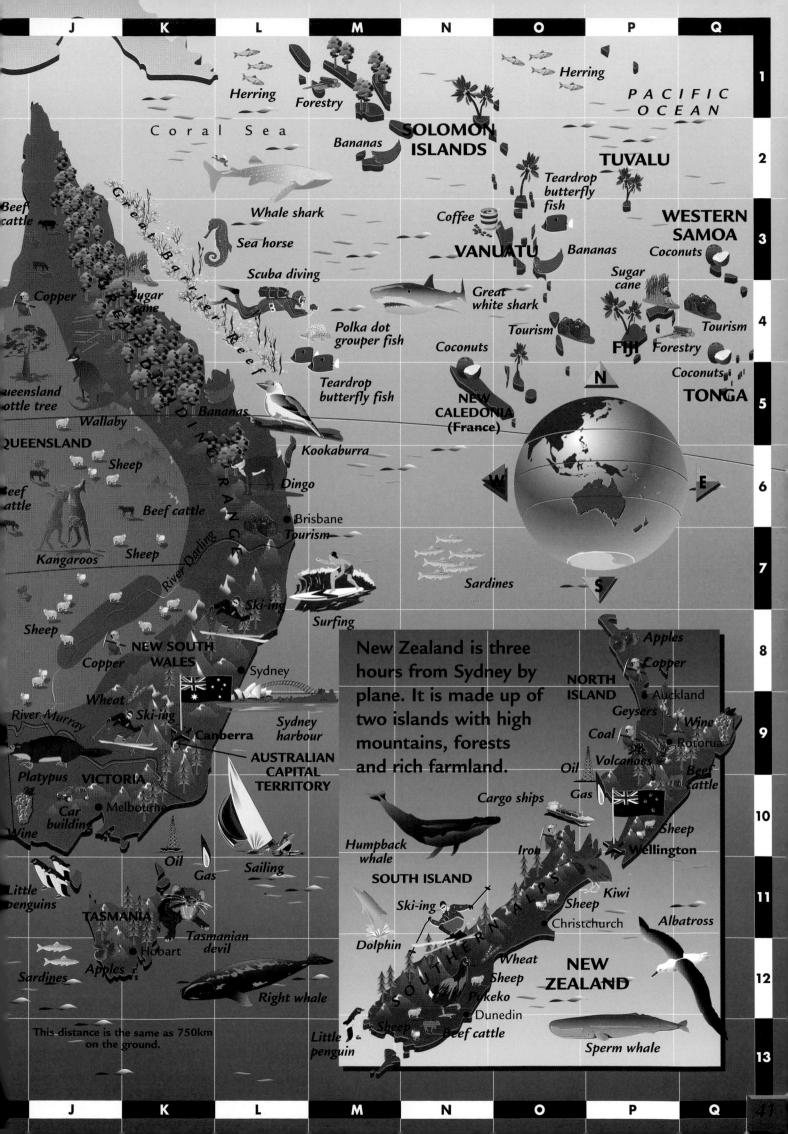

1
2
3
4
5
6
7
8
9
10
11
12
13

Herring

Forestry

Coral Sea

Bananas

SOLOMON ISLANDS

Herring

PACIFIC OCEAN

TUVALU

Teardrop butterfly fish

Coffee

WESTERN SAMOA

Beef cattle

Whale shark

VANUATU

Bananas

Coconuts

Sea horse

Great Barrier Reef

Copper

Sugar cane

Scuba diving

Great white shark

Sugar cane

Tourism

Polka dot grouper fish

Coconuts

Tourism

FIJI

Forestry

Queensland bottle tree

Teardrop butterfly fish

Coconuts

TONGA

Wallaby

N

Bananas

NEW CALEDONIA (France)

QUEENSLAND

Kookaburra

W   E

Sheep

Beef cattle

Dingo

Beef cattle

Brisbane
Tourism

Sardines

S

Sheep

Kangaroos

Sheep

Surfing

Ski-ing

Apples

Copper

Sheep

NORTH ISLAND

NEW SOUTH WALES

Auckland

Copper

Sydney

Geysers

Wine

New Zealand is three hours from Sydney by plane. It is made up of two islands with high mountains, forests and rich farmland.

Coal

Rotorua

Wheat

Sydney harbour

Volcanoes

River Murray

Ski-ing

Canberra

Oil

Beef cattle

AUSTRALIAN CAPITAL TERRITORY

Gas

Platypus

VICTORIA

Cargo ships

Wellington

Sheep

Car building

Melbourne

Iron

Wine

Humpback whale

Oil

Gas

Sailing

SOUTH ISLAND

Kiwi

Little penguins

Ski-ing

Sheep

Christchurch

Albatross

TASMANIA

Dolphin

SOUTHERN ALPS

NEW ZEALAND

Tasmanian devil

Hobart

Wheat

Sheep

Apples

Pukeko

Sardines

Sheep

Dunedin

Right whale

Beef cattle

This distance is the same as 750km on the ground.

Little penguin

Sperm whale

Gazetteer

On these pages, you can discover interesting facts about the world. Look up the names of the places in the index and find out where they are on the maps in this atlas.

Where in the world is...

...the hottest place?
Dallol in Ethiopia, which has an average temperature of 34°C (94°F).

In Dallol, you could fry an egg on a sun-baked rock.

...the coldest place?
Vostock in Antarctica. The lowest temperature ever recorded was -89°C (-128°F), which is over three times as cold as inside a deep freeze.

...the wettest place?
Mawsynram in India, where nearly 12m of rain falls each year. This is enough to cover a three-storey building.

...the driest place?
Atacama Desert in Chile, where it has rained only a few times in the last 400 years.

Which country is the...

...biggest country?
Russia, which is 17,075,400sq km.

...smallest country?
Vatican City, which is 0.44sq km.

If Russia were the size of a soccer pitch, the Vatican City would be the size of a small stamp.

...emptiest country?
Mongolia, which has a huge desert and high mountains. There are only a few towns which are far apart.

...most crowded country?
Monaco, which is a tiny country in Europe. It has an orchestra larger than its army.

Where is the...

...highest mountain in the world?
Mount Everest in the Himalayas in Nepal. It is 8,848m high, which is over nine times as tall as the highest waterfall in the world.
8,848m

...highest waterfall in the world?
Angel Falls in Venezuela. It has a total drop of 979m. It is over twice as high as the tallest building in North America.
979m

...highest geyser in the world?
Waimangu Geyser, in New Zealand. It once shot out a jet of water 460m high, slightly taller than Sears Tower.
460m

...highest building in North America?
Sears Tower, USA. It is 443m tall, nearly four times taller than the tallest tree.
443m

...highest tree in the world?
A redwood tree in California, USA. It is 111.56m, over 40 times taller than the tallest person in the world.
111.56m

Who was the world's tallest person?
An American called Robert Pershing Wadlow was the world's tallest person. He was 2.72m tall.

FACT FINDER

Find these record-breaking places in the atlas.

▶ The highest mountain (page 34, square J 8)

▶ The tallest waterfall (page 20, square E 4)

▶ The longest river (page 31, square L 7)

▶ The driest place (page 21, square E 9)

W

E

London

New York

Tokyo

What time is it?

Across the world, at the same moment, clocks show different times. This is because the world is divided into time zones. All time is measured from Greenwich, London, UK. When you cross a time zone to the east of Greenwich, time is one hour ahead. When you cross a time zone to the west of Greenwich, time is one hour behind.

The letters *am* stand for ante meridian, which means the hours from midnight until mid-day, or the morning. The letters *pm* stand for post meridian, which means the hours from mid-day until midnight, or the afternoon and evening.

If it is 12pm in London, what time is it in New York and Tokyo?

Land and sea

Imagine the world as a cake. Most of the cake would be oceans and seas, and one small slice would be the land. Most of the slice of land would be desert, rainforest, mountains, ice and grassland. Less than half the slice would be places where people can live and farm. In this atlas, you can find the biggest rainforest on page 20, see square H 5, and the biggest desert on page 30, see square E 5.

Which are the three longest rivers?

The River Nile in North Africa is 6,670km long. It would take you over four months to walk from one end to the other.

The River Amazon in South America is 6,430km long. It would take you over two months to run along its length.

The River Yangtze in China is 6,300km long. You could cycle very fast from one end to the other in just over one month.

*I*ndex

This index lists all the places on the maps in this atlas. The page number tells you which map to go to and the grid reference tells you where the place is on the map. You can find out how to use grid references on page 9.

*A*bidjan p30 D10
Abu Dhabi p29 J11
Abuja p30 G9
Acapulco p18 E9
Accra p30 E10
Addis Ababa p31 N9
Adelaide p40 I9
Aden p29 F15
Afghanistan p11, p34 A7
Africa p4, p30-33, p43
Ahaggar Mountains
  p30 F5
Ahmadabad p35 E10
Al Basrah p28 G9
Al Rub al Khali
  see Empty Quarter
Alabama p17 M7
Alaska p10, p12 D4,
  p16 C3
Albania p11, p25 M7
Alberta p14 G8
Alexandria p30 L4
Algeria p10, p30 E4
Algiers p30 F2
Alice Springs p40 G5
Alma-Ata p26 G10
Alps p22 H13, p24 H5
Altai Mountains p36 F3
Altay Mountains p27 J9
Amman p28 D8
Amsterdam p22 G10
An Nafud
  see Great Sandy Desert
Anchorage p16 C4
Andaman Islands p11,
  p35 M13
Andes Mountains p21 F9
Andorra p10, p24 F6
Angola p10, p33 C11
Anguilla p10, p19 P8
Ankara p28 C5
Antananarivo p33 L12
Antarctic Circle p4, p7,
  p13 N11
Antarctica p4, p10,
  p13, p42
Antigua p10, p19 P9
Appalachian Mountains
  p17 N6
Arabian Desert p29 F12

Arabian Sea p29 J14
Aral Sea p26 E9
Archangel p26 F4
Arctic p7, p12
Arctic Circle p4, p6, p7,
  p12 C11 & G6, p14 K6,
  p16 C3, p22 B2 & H3,
  p26 E2 & O2, p27 O3
Arctic Ocean p4, p10,
  p12 E9, p14 G1, p26 G2
Argentina p10, p21 G12
Arizona p16 G8
Arkansas p17 L7
Armenia p11, p26 C9
Ashgabat p26 D11
Asia p4, p28-29, p34-39
Asmera p31 N8
Asunción p21 H10
Atacama Desert p21 E9,
  p42
Athens p25 O9
Atlantic Ocean p4, p10,
  p12 A10, p13 K5, p15
  P6, p17 P6, p19 N6,
  p21 I13, p22 A7, p24
  B3, p30 C2, p33 A10
Atlas Mountains p30 D3
Auckland p41 P9
Austin p17 K9
Australia p4, p11, p40-41
Australian Capital
  Territory p41 K9
Austria p11, p23 I12
Azerbaijan p11, p26 C9
Azores p10

*B*affin Bay p12 C8
Baffin Island p12 C7,
  p15 K4
Baghdad p28 F8
Bahamas p10, p19 L7
Bahrain p11, p29 H11
Baja California p18 A3
Baku p26 C9
Bali p39 I11
Baltic Sea p23 K8
Baltimore p17 O5
Bamako p30 C8

Bandar Seri Begawan
  p38 H8
Bangalore p35 G14
Bangkok p38 D6
Bangladesh p11, p35 K10
Bangui p32 D6
Banjul p30 A8
Banks Island p14 G4
Barbados p10, p19 Q10
Barbuda p10, p19 P9
Barcelona p24 F7
Barren Desert p28 K8
Bay of Biscay p22 C12
Beijing p37 K6
Beirut p28 D7
Belarus p11, p26 C5
Belfast p22 D8
Belgium p10, p22 F10
Belgrade p25 M5
Belize p10, p18 H10
Belmopan p18 H9
Benin p10, p30 E9
Bergen p22 G6
Bering Sea p27 P2
Berlin p23 I10
Bermuda p10
Bern p22 G13
Bhutan p11, p34 K8
Bishkek p26 G10
Bissau p30 A8
Black Sea p25 Q6,
  p26 B7, p28 D4
Bogotá p20 C4
Bolivia p10, p20 F8
Bombay p35 E12
Bordeaux p22 D13
Borneo p38 H10
Bosnia-Herzegovina
  p11, p25 L5
Boston p17 P3
Botswana p10, p33 D13
Brasília p20 J7
Bratislava p23 J12
Brazil p10, p20 H6, p42
Brazzaville p32 C8
Brisbane p41 L6
British Columbia p14 E9
Brunei p11, p38 G8
Brussels p22 F10
Bucharest p25 P5

Budapest p23 K13
Buenos Aires p21 H12
Bujumbura p32 F8
Bulgaria p11, p25 O6
Burkina Faso p10,
  p30 E8
Burundi p11, p32 G8

*C*abinda p10, p32 B8
Cairo p31 L4
Calcutta p35 K10
Cali p20 B5
California p16 E6, p42
Cambodia p11, p38 D7
Cameroon p10, p32 B6
Canada p10, p12 C5,
  p14-15
Canary Islands p10,
  p30 B4
Canberra p41 K9
Cape Horn p21 G17
Cape of Good Hope
  p33 D17
Cape Town p33 D16
Cape Verde Islands p10
Caracas p20 D3
Cardiff p22 D9
Caribbean p19
Caribbean Sea p19 K10,
  p20 A2
Caroline Islands p11
Casablanca p30 D2
Caspian Sea p26 C9,
  p28 H3
Cayenne p20 H3
Central African Republic
  p10, p32 C5
Central America p18-19
Chad p10, p31 I8
Chang Jiang
  see River Yangtze
Chengdu p36 I9
Cherskiy Mountains
  p27 N4
Chicago p17 M5
Chile p10, p21 E13, p42
China p11, p36 G8, p43
Chisinau p26 B6

Chittagong p35 L10
Christchurch p41 O11
Cleveland p17 N4
Cochin p35 F15
Colombia p10, p20 C5
Colombo p35 H16
Colorado p16 H5
Colorado River p16 F7
Columbus p17 N5
Comoros p11, p33 K10
Conakry p30 B9
Congo p10, p32 C7
Congo, Democratic
  Republic of p10, p32 E8
Connecticut p17 P3
Coober Pedy p40 H8
Copenhagen p22 I8
Coral Sea p41 K2
Corsica p11, p24 H7
Costa Rica p10, p19 J13
Crete p11, p25 P11
Croatia p11, p25 L5
Cuba p10, p19 J8
Curaçao p19 N11
Cyprus p11, p28 C7
Czech Republic p11,
  p23 J11

*D*akar p30 A7
Dalian p37 L6
Dallas p17 K8
Damascus p28 D8
Dar es Salaam p32 J9
Darwin p40 G2
Dasht-E Kavir
  see Salt Desert
Dasht-E Lut
  see Barren Desert
Dead Sea p28 C8
Delaware p17 P5
Denmark p11, p22 H8
Denver p16 I5
Detroit p17 N4
Dhaka p34 K9
Djibouti (city) p31 O9
Djibouti (country) p11,
  p31 N8
Dodoma p32 H8
Doha p29 I11
Dominica p10, p19 Q9
Dominican Republic p10,
  p19 M8
Dubai p29 J11
Dublin p22 D8
Dubrovnik p25 M6
Dunedin p41 N13
Durban p33 G15
Dushanbe p26 F11

*E*ast China Sea p37 N8
Eastern Asia p36-37
Ecuador p10, p20 B6
Edinburgh p22 E8
Edmonton p14 G9
Egypt p11, p31 K5
El Aaiún p30 C4
El Paso p16 H8
El Salvador p10, p18 H11
Elburz Mountains p28 G7
Ellesmere Island p12 C7,
  p15 K1
Empty Quarter p29 H13
Equator p4, p6, p7, p20
  I4, p31 P12, p32 M7,
  p35 M17, p39 N6
Equatorial Guinea p10,
  p32 A7
Eritrea p11, p31 M7
Estonia p10, p23 M7
Ethiopia p11, p31 M10,
  p42
Ethiopian Highlands
  p31 N10
Europe p4, p22-26

*F*alkland Islands p10,
  p21 I15
Federal Republic of
  Yugoslavia p11, p25 M5
Fiji p11, p41 P4
Finland p10, p23 L4
Flores p39 K11
Florida p17 O9
Fort Worth p17 K8
France p10, p22 E12,
  p24 E4
Frankfurt p22 H11
Freetown p30 B9
French Guiana p10,
  p20 H3
Fuzhou p37 M10

*G*abon p10, p32 A7
Gaborone p33 F14
Galapagos Islands p10,
  p21 A10
Gambia p10, p30 B8
Genoa p24 I5
Georgetown p20 F3
Georgia p11, p17 N7,
  p26 C8
Germany p11, p22 G10
Ghana p10, p30 D9
Gibraltar p24 B9
Gobi Desert p36 H4
Göteborg p22 I7
Great Barrier Reef p41 K3
Great Bear Lake p14 G5

Great Dividing Range
  p41 J4
Great Salt Lake p16 G5
Great Sandy Desert
  p29 E10
Great Slave Lake p14 G7
Great Victoria Desert
  p40 F8
Greater Antilles p19 J8
Greece p11, p25 N8
Greenland p10, p12 C9,
  p15 L1
Grenada p10, p19 Q11
Grenadines p10, p19 Q10
Guadeloupe p10, p19 Q9
Guam p11
Guangzhou p37 K11
Guatemala p10, p18 G10
Guatemala City p18 G10
Guinea p10, p30 B9
Guinea-Bissau p10,
  p30 A8
Gulf of Alaska p16 C6
Gulf of Mexico p17 L10,
  p18 G6
Gulf of Oman p29 K11
Gulf of St Lawrence
  p15 P10
Guyana p10, p20 F3

*H*ainan p37 K13
Haiti p10, p19 M9
Hanoi p38 D4
Harare p33 G12
Harbin p37 M3
Havana p19 J8
Hawaii p16 C11
Helsinki p23 L6
Himalayan
  Mountains p34 G7,
  p36 C8, p42
Hiroshima p37 O6
Ho Chi Minh City p38 E7
Hobart p41 K12
Hokkaido p37 O3
Honduras p10, p19 I10
Hong Kong p11, p37 L11
Honshu p37 P4
Houston p17 K9
Huang He
  see Yellow River
Hudson Bay p12 A7,
  p15 K8
Hungary p11, p23 K13
Hyderabad p35 G12

*I*biza p24 E9
Iceland p10, p12 C11,
  p22 B2

Idaho p16 G4
Illinois p17 L5
India p11, p35 G10, p42
Indian Ocean p11, p13
  P6, p31 P12, p33 J9,
  p35 I14, p38 B7, p40 B6
Indiana p17 M5
Indianapolis p17 M5
Indonesia p11, p38 G10
Iowa p17 K5
Iran p11, p28 J8
Iraq p11, p28 F7
Irian Jaya p11, p39 N7
Irkutsk p27 K9
Isfahan p28 I8
Islamabad p34 E6
Israel p11, p28 C8
Istanbul p25 Q7, p28 B5
Italy p11, p25 J6
Ivory Coast p10, p30 C10

*J*acksonville p17 O8
Jakarta p38 G12
Jamaica p10, p19 K9
Japan p11, p37 O5
Java p38 G12
Jerusalem p28 C8
Jiddah p29 D12
Johannesburg p33 F14
Jordan p11, p28 D8

*K*2 (Mt Godwin
  Austen) p36 C7
Kabul p34 D6
Kalahari Desert p33 D13
Kaliningrad p23 K9,
  p26 C4
Kampala p32 H7
Kanpur p34 G9
Kansas p17 J6
Kansas City p17 K6
Kara Kum Desert
  p26 D10
Karachi p35 C10
Karakoram Range p34 E5
Kathmandu p34 I8
Kazakhstan p11, p26 E8
Kentucky p17 M6
Kenya p11, p32 I6
Khartoum p31 L8
Kiev p26 C6
Kigali p32 G7
Kingston p19 L9
Kinshasa p32 C8
Kiribati p11
Kjølen Mountains p23 J4
Kolyma Mountains
  p27 O3
Kuala Lumpur p38 E9

Kuwait (city) p29 H9
Kuwait (country) p11,
  p29 F9
Kyoto p37 O6
Kyrgyzstan p11, p26 G11
Kyushu p37 O7

*L*a Paz p20 E8
Lagos p30 F10
Lahore p34 E7
Lake Baikal p27 L8
Lake Chad p30 H8
Lake Erie p15 L13
Lake Eyre p40 H8
Lake Huron p15 L12
Lake Michigan p15 K13
Lake Nasser p31 L6
Lake Nyasa p33 H10
Lake Ontario p15 M12
Lake Superior p15 K12
Lake Tanganyika p32 G8
Lake Titicaca p20 D8
Lake Victoria p32 H7
Lake Volta p30 E10
Laos p11, p38 C5
Lapland p23 K2
Latvia p10, p11, p23 K8
Lebanon p11, p28 C8
Lesotho p10, p33 F15
Lesser Antilles p19 O10
Liberia p10, p30 B10
Libreville p32 A7
Libya p10, p30 H4
Liechtenstein p11,
  p22 H13
Lilongwe p33 H11
Lima p20 C8
Lisbon p24 A7
Lithuania p11, p23 K8
Ljubljana p25 K4
Lomé p30 E10
London p22 E10, p43
Los Angeles p16 E7
Louisiana p17 L8
Luanda p33 B9
Lusaka p33 F11
Luxembourg (city)
  p22 G11
Luxembourg (country)
  p22 G11, p11
Luzon p38 G4
Lyon p24 G4

*M*acau p11
Macedonia p11, p25 N7
Madagascar p11,
  p33 K12
Madeira p10, p30 B2
Madras p35 H14

Madrid p24 C7
Magadan p27 O5
Maine p17 P2
Majorca p24 E8
Malabo p32 A6
Malawi p11, p33 H11
Malaysia p11, p38 E8
Maldive Islands p11,
  p35 E17
Mali p10, p30 D6
Malmö p23 I8
Malta p10, p25 K10
Maluku p39 K8
Managua p18 I11
Manila p38 H4
Manitoba p15 I9
Maputo p33 H14
Marrakech p30 D3
Marseille p24 G6
Marshall Islands p11
Martinique p10, p19 Q10
Maryland p17 P5
Maseru p33 F15
Mashad p28 L6
Massachusetts p17 P3
Mauritania p10, p30 B6
Mauritius p33 M13
Mayotte p11, p33 K10
Mbabane p33 G14
Mecca p29 E12
Medina p29 E11
Mediterranean Sea
  p24 F9, p28 A7, p30 F1
Melbourne p41 J10
Memphis p17 M7
Mexico p10, p18 D6
Mexico City p18 E8
Michigan p17 M4
Micronesia, States of p11
Middle East p28, p29
Milan p24 I5
Milwaukee p17 M4
Mindanao p39 J6
Minnesota p17 K2
Minorca p24 G8
Minsk p26 C5
Mississippi p17 M7
Mississippi River p17 L7
Missouri p17 L6
Missouri River p17 K5
Mogadishu p31 P11
Moldova p11, p26 B6
Monaco p11, p24 H6,
  p42
Mongolia p11, p36 H4
Monrovia p30 B10
Montana p16 H3
Montevideo p21 I12
Montreal p15 N12
Morocco p10, p30 D3
Moscow p26 D5
Mozambique p11,
  p33 H13

Mt Aconcagua p21 F12
Mt Ararat p28 F5
Mt Elbrus p26 C8
Mt Erebus p13 N10
Mt Etna p25 K9
Mt Everest p34 J8,
  p36 D9, p42
Mt Fuji p37 P5
Mt Glittertinden p22 H5
Mt Godwin Austen see K2
Mt Kilimanjaro p32 H8
Mt Logan p14 D6
Mt McKinley p16 C4
Mt Olympus p25 N8
Mt Rushmore p17 I4
Mt Vesuvius p25 K8
Murmansk p26 F3
Muscat p29 L11
Myanmar p11, p38 A4

N'Djamena p30 H9
Nagasaki p37 O7
Nagpur p35 G11
Nairobi p32 I7
Namib Desert p33 B12
Namibia p10, p33 C12
Naples p25 K8
Nashville p17 M6
Nauru p11
Nebraska p17 I5
Nepal p11, p34 H8, p42
Netherlands p10, p22 G9
Nevada p16 F6
Nevis p10, p19 P9
New Brunswick p15 O11
New Caledonia p11,
  p41 N5
New Delhi p34 F8
New Hampshire p17 P3
New Jersey p17 P4
New Mexico p16 H7
New Orleans p17 M8
New South Wales p41 K8
New York p17 O3,
  p17 P4, p43
New Zealand p11,
  p41 O12, p42
Newfoundland p15 P8
Niamey p30 E8
Nicaragua p10, p19 I11
Nicobar Islands p11,
  p35 M15
Nicosia p28 C7
Niger p10, p30 G6
Nigeria p10, p30 G10
Nizhniy Novgorod p26 E6
North America p4,
  p14-17
North Carolina p17 O6
North Dakota p17 J3

North Island p41 O8
North Korea p11, p37 M4
North Pacific Ocean
  p39 L5
North Pole p6, p12 E8
North Sea p22 F7
Northern Africa p30-31
Northern Europe p22-23
Northern Ireland p22 D8
Northern Marianas p11
Northern Territory
  p40 G4
Northwest Territories
  p14 G6
Norway p10, p12 D12,
  p22 H7
Norwegian Sea p23 J1
Nouakchott p30 A6
Nova Scotia p15 P11

*O*hio p17 N5
Ohio River p17 M6
Okhotsk p27 O6
Oklahoma p17 J7
Oklahoma City p17 K7
Oman p11, p29 K13
Ontario p15 J10
Oran p30 E2
Oregon p16 E3
Oslo p22 I6
Ottawa p15 M12
Ouagadougou p30 E8

*P*acific Islands p41
Pacific Ocean p10, p11,
  p13 J7, p14 A8, p16
  D11, p18 A7, p21 B12,
  p27 P13, p37 P8,
  p41 P1
Pakistan p11, p34 C8
Palau p11
Palermo p25 K9
Panama p10, p19 J13
Panama Canal p19 K12
Panama City p19 K12
Papua New Guinea p11,
  p39 O8
Paraguay p10, p21 G9
Paramaribo p20 G3
Paris p22 F11, p24 G2
Parry Islands p14 H3
Pennsylvania p17 N4
Persian Gulf p29 H10
Perth p40 C9
Peru p10, p20 C7
Philadelphia p17 P4
Philippines p11, p38 H5
Phnom Penh p38 E7
Phoenix p16 G7

Poland p11, p23 K10
Pontine Mountains
  p28 E5
Port Moresby p39 P8
Port-au-Prince p19 M9
Porto p24 B6
Porto-Novo p30 E10
Portugal p10, p24 A6
Prague p23 I11
Pretoria p33 F14
Prince Edward Island
  p15 P11
Prince of Wales
  Island p15 I4
Príncipe p10, p30 F12
Puerto Rico p10, p19 O9
Pyongyang p37 M5
Pyrenees p24 D6

Qatar p11, p29 I11
Qingdao p37 L6
Quebec p15 N9
Queen Elizabeth
  Islands p15 J2
Queensland p41 I5
Quetta p34 C8
Quito p20 B5

Rabat p30 D2
Recife p20 M5
Red Sea p29 C10,
  p31 M5
Republic of Ireland p10,
  p22 B8
Republic of South
  Africa p10, p33 D14
Réunion p33 M13
Reykjavík p22 B3
Rhode Island p17 P3
Riga p23 L8
Rio de Janeiro p20 K9
Rio Grande p16 I8,
  p18 E4
River Amazon p20 F5,
  p43
River Amu Darya p26 E11
River Amur p27 O8
River Brahmaputra
  p34 K8
River Danube p23 I12,
  p25 O5
River Darling p41 K7
River Don p26 D7
River Elbe p22 H9
River Euphrates p28 E6
River Ganges p35 H9
River Godavari p35 G11
River Helmand p34 B7
River Indus p34 D8
River Irrawaddy P38 B5

River Irtysh p26 H9
River Kasai p32 C8
River Lena p27 L5
River Loire p22 D12,
  p24 F3
River Mackenzie p14 F5
River Mekong p38 D5
River Murray p41 I9
River Narmada p35 E10
River Nelson p15 J9
River Niger p30 F9
River Nile p31 L7, p43
River Ob p26 H6
River Orange p33 C15
River Orinoco p20 D3
River Paraná p21 H11
River Po p25 J5
River Rhine p22 G11
River Rhône p22 F13,
  p24 G5
River São Francisco
  p20 K7
River Seine p22 F12,
  p24 G3
River St Lawrence
  p15 N11
River Tagus p24 C7
River Tigris p28 F7
River Volga p26 D7
River Yangtze p37 I9, p43
River Yenisey p27 J6
River Yukon p14 E5
River Zaire p32 E7
River Zambezi p33 E11
Riyadh p29 G11
Rocky Mountains p14 E6,
  p16 G3
Romania p11, p25 N4
Rome p25 J7
Ronne Ice Shelf p13 L7
Ross Ice Shelf p13 M9
Ross Sea p13 M10
Rotorua p41 P9
Russia p11, p12 H8,
  p26 G7, p27, p42
Rwanda p11, p32 F7
Ryukyu Islands p11,
  p37 O8

Sahara Desert p30 E5
Sakhalin Island p27 P7
Salt Desert p28 J7
San Antonio p17 K9
San Diego p16 F7
San Francisco p16 E6
San Jose p16 E16
San José p19 J12
San Juan p19 O9
San Marino p11, p25 J6
San Salvador p18 H11
Sana p29 F14
Santiago p21 F12

Santo Domingo p19 N9
São Paulo p21 K9
São Tomé p10, p30 F11
Sapporo p37 P3
Sarajevo p25 M6
Sardinia p11, p24 H8
Saskatchewan p14 G9
Saudi Arabia p11,
  p29 F12
Sea of Japan p37 O3
Sea of Okhotsk p27 O6
Seattle p16 E2
Senegal p10, p30 A7
Seoul p37 N6
Serbia see Federal
  Republic of Yugoslavia
Seville p24 B8
Seychelles p11, p32 L8
Shanghai p37 M8
Shenyang p37 M5
Shikoku p37 O6
Siberia p27 M7
Sicily p11, p25 K9
Sierra Leone p10, p30 B9
Sierra Madre p18 C4
Singapore p11, p38 F9
Skopje p25 N7
Slovakia p11, p23 K12
Slovenia p11, p25 K5
Socotra p11, p29 J16
Sofia p25 N6
Solomon Islands p11,
  p41 N2
Somalia p11, p31 P9
South America p4, p9,
  p20-21, p43
South Australia p40 G7
South Carolina p17 O7
South China Sea
  p37 M12, p38 E3
South Dakota p17 I4
South Georgia p10
South Island p41 M11
South Korea p11, p37 M6
South Pole p6, p13 M8
South-east Asia p38-39
South-west Asia p28-29
Southern Africa p32-33
Southern Alps p41 N12
Southern Asia p34-35
Southern Europe p24-25
Spain p10, p24 C8
Sri Lanka p11, p35 I15
St Kitts p10, p19 P9
St Louis p17 I6
St Lucia p10, p19 Q10
St Petersburg p26 D4
St Vincent p10, p19 Q10
Stockholm p23 J7
Sudan p11, p31 K8
Suez Canal p31 M4
Sulawesi p39 J9
Sumatra p38 E10

Sumba p39 J11
Surinam p10, p20 G3
Svalbard Islands p12 E10
Swaziland p11, p33 G14
Sweden p10, p11,
  p12 D12, p23 J5
Switzerland p11, p22 G13
Sydney p41 L8
Syria p11, p28 D7

Tabriz p28 G6
Taipei p37 M10
Taiwan p11, p37 M10
Tajikistan p11, p26 G11
Takla Makan Desert
  p36 D6
Tallinn p23 L6
Tanami Desert p40 G5
Tanzania p11, p33 H9
Tashkent p26 F10
Tasmania p11, p41 J11
Taurus Mountains p28 C6
Tbilisi p26 C8
Tegucigalpa p18 H11
Tehran p28 I7
Tel Aviv p28 C8
Tennessee p17 M7
Texas p17 J9
Thailand p11, p38 C5
Thar Desert p34 D8
Thimpu p34 K8
Tianjin p37 K6
Tibet p36 E7
Tien Shan Mountains
  p36 D4
Tierra del Fuego p21 H16
Timor p39 K11
Tiranë p25 M7
Tobago p10, p19 Q11
Togo p10, p30 E9
Tokyo p37 P5, p43
Tonga p41 Q5
Toronto p15 M12
Trinidad p10, p19 Q11
Tripoli p30 H3
Trondheim p22 I4
Tropic of Cancer p6, p7,
  p17 L11, p19 N7,
  p29 A11, p30 A5,
  p32 I1, p35 A10,
  p37 Q9, p38 D3
Tropic of Capricorn p6,
  p7, p21 D10, p33 A13,
  p39 Q13, p40 B6
Tunis p30 H2
Tunisia p10, p30 G3
Turin p24 H5
Turkey p11, p25 P7,
  p28 D5
Turkmenistan p11,
  p26 E11
Tuvalu p11, p41 P3

*U*ganda p11, p32 G6
Ukraine p11, p26 C6
Ulan Bator p36 I3
United Arab Emirates p11,
　p29 I11
United Kingdom p10,
　p22 E8
United States p10,
　p16-17, p42
Ural Mountains p26 F7
Uruguay p10, p21 I11
Utah p16 G6
Uzbekistan p11, p26 E10

*V*ancouver p14 E10
Vanuatu p11, p41 N3
Vatican City p11,
　p25 J7, p42

Venezuela p10,
　p20 D3, p42
Venice p25 J5
Verkhoyausk
　Mountains p27 M5
Vermont p17 P3
Victoria Island p12 C6,
　p14 H5
Victoria p41 J10
Vienna p23 J12
Vientiane p38 D5
Vietnam p11, p38 E5
Vilnius p23 L9
Vinhdaya Range p35 F10
Virgin Islands p10,
　p19 P9
Virginia p17 O5
Vishakhapatnam p35 I12
Vladivostok p27 O10
Volgograd p26 D7

*W*arsaw p23 K10
Washington p16 E2
Washington DC p17 O5
Weddell Sea p13 K6
Wellington p41 P10
West Virginia p17 O5
Western Australia p40 D8
Western Sahara p10,
　p30 B5, p42
Western Samoa p41 Q3
Windhoek p33 C13
Winnipeg p15 J11
Wisconsin p17 L4
Wyoming p16 H4

*X*ian p37 J8

*Y*ablonovyy
　Mountains p27 I8
Yangon p38 B6
Yaoundé p32 B6
Yellow River p37 K7
Yellow Sea p37 M7
Yemen p11, p29 H14
Yerevan p26 C9
Yukon River p16 C3
Yukon Territory p14 E5

*Z*agreb p25 L4
Zagros Mountains
　p28 H7
Zambia p10, p33 E11
Zanzibar Island p32 J8
Zimbabwe p11, p33 F12

*T*roubleshooting tips

System requirements

The Atlas disk will work on most Windows or Apple Macintosh computers.
To check that it will run on yours, please read the minimum specifications below.

- **Windows**

  486DX/33Mhz PC with Windows version 3.1, 3.11, 95 (or later); SVGA colour
  monitor; Soundblaster-compatible soundcard; 8Mb RAM (16Mb RAM
  recommended with Windows 95)

- **Macintosh**

  Apple Macintosh with 68020 processor (or greater), system 7.0 (or later) and
  8Mb of RAM.

Quick fixes

To get the most out of your Atlas disk, please check:
1. Your monitor is set to 640 x 480 and 256 colours.
2. You have the Arial font (Windows users) or Helvetica font (Macintosh users)
installed in your fonts folder.
3. You have no other applications open.

Read me file

If you have a problem with your Atlas disk that is not covered in the notes above,
be sure to check the Read me file. You can open the Read me file by clicking on
the Read me icon which you will find next to the Atlas icon.

Helpline

You can call the helpline on 0171 684 4050. The lines are open from 10.00 am to
5.00 pm, Monday to Friday, and calls are charged at normal rates. But remember
to get permission from the person who pays the bill before you use the phone.

Created and published by
Two-Can Publishing Ltd
346 Old Street
London
EC1V 9NQ

Disk
Creative Director: Jason Page
Programming Director: Paul Steven
Art Director: Sarah Evans
Senior Designer: James Evans
Editors: Rob Mitchell, Lyndall Thomas
Programmer: Roger Emery
Authors: Jason Page, Rob Mitchell,
Lyndall Thomas, Lucy Arnold
Illustrators: Jon Stuart, James Jarvis,
Mel Pickering
Production Director: Lorraine Estelle
Production Controller: KatherineHarvey
Project Manager: Joya Bart-Plange

Book
Text: Andrew Solway
Consultant: Steve Watts
Computer Illustrations: Mel Pickering,
Jacqueline Land
Editors: Deborah Kespert, Kate Asser,
Editoral Support: Claire Llewellyn,
Julia Hillyard, Claire Yude
Art Director: Belinda Webster
Senior Designer: Helen Holmes
Designer: Michele Egar

This edition published in 1998 by Two-Can
Publishing Ltd.

ISBN 1-85434-630-X

Dewey Decimal Classification 912

A catalogue record for this book is available
from the British Library

Hardback 4 6 8 10 9 7 5 3

Photographic Credits: ZEFA: p7;
John Englefield: p9

Printed in Hong Kong

CHECK OUT THE WHOLE INTERFACT RANGE

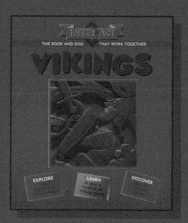
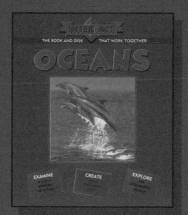

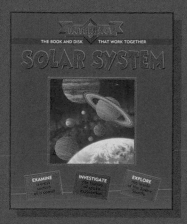
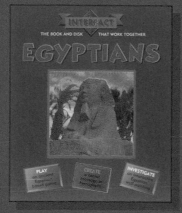

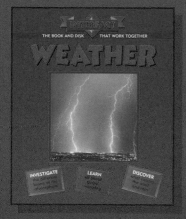
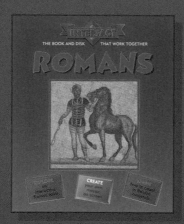

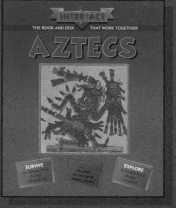

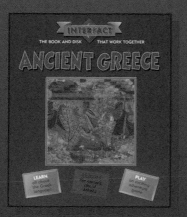